The GENESIS

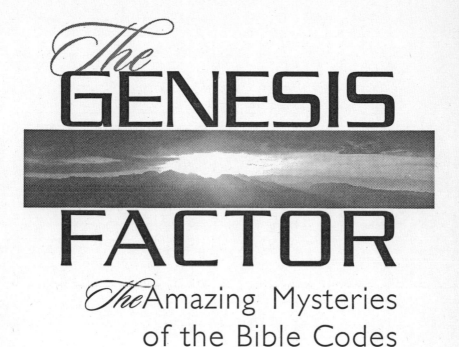

FACTOR

The Amazing Mysteries of the Bible Codes

Yacov Rambsel

LIONS
HEAD

THE GENESIS FACTOR

ISBN: 1-891668-06-4
Published by Lion's Head Publishing, Beverly Hills, CA
Cover design by Koechel Peterson & Associates,
Minneapolis, Minnesota
Manufactured in the United States of America

CONTENTS

A SPECIAL INTRODUCTION BY DR. PAUL CROUCH SR.

You are holding in your hand not just another book, but a veritable nuclear bomb! The fuse on this cataclysm is poised to blow into oblivion the theories and arguments of all the silly critics, doubters, agnostics, atheists, and other enemies of the almighty God! The Holy Bible grants only eleven words out of 773,692 to address these pitiful souls: "The fool hath said in his heart, there is no God" (Psalm 14:1).

First of all, God needs no defense—He is God—period. In Matthew 24:35, He says: "Heaven and earth shall pass away; but my words shall not pass away." But because He is a God of infinite love, He literally moves heaven and earth to reveal Himself and His love to all mankind. The apostle Paul writes: "For the invisible things of him from the creation of the world are clearly seen, being understood by the things that are made, even his eternal power and Godhead; so that they are without excuse" (Romans 1:20). Hugh Ross, in his book *The Fingerprint of God*, gives numerous examples of the Creator's amazing handiwork that prove to any honest seeker the awesome design of a divine, intelligent creator.

But, wonders of wonders, God has given to this terminal generation yet another explosive example and proof of His amazing

7

pursuit of the souls of mankind—His divine and highest creation! The ELS (Equidistant Letter Sequence) phenomenon is literally blowing the minds of some of our worst critics. For example, in the "Suffering Servant" passage of Isaiah 53, where we read: "He was wounded for our transgressions, he was bruised for our iniquities: the chastisement of our peace was upon him; and with his stripes we are healed" (Isaiah 53:5), every twentieth letter spells "JESUS IS MY NAME." When the critics countered by saying YESHUA (the Hebrew name for Jesus) simply and literally means "salvation," we looked again and found "NAZARENE" in the same chapter along with seventy-four of the names, places, and events of the time period of Jesus of Nazareth! After these irrefutable revelations, the critics are silent and simply refuse to discuss this passage at all!

Finally, our critics attempted to show that this ELS phenomenon was simply a chance occurrence that could be found in other great works of literature. Shakespearean literature, *War and Peace,* and other great writings were examined. To the chagrin of the scholars, of the hundreds and even thousands of sequences that were examined, only a few chance words and names were discovered at ELS. These findings could not compare with the hundreds of names, places, and whole sentences found in unbroken sequences in the Holy Bible, such as Isaiah 53.

Ah, dear reader, friend or foe, I plead with you to read this explosive volume with an open mind. Examine the evidence for yourself. To critics, I say that if you still do not believe, you will have to CHOOSE NOT TO BELIEVE in spite of the evidence from these ancient writings that are thousands of years old. To believers, you will be thrilled and encouraged in your "faith which was once delivered unto the saints" (Jude 1:3). You will look forward with even greater joy to the glorious reward that awaits "those who love Him"!

FOREWORD

ow does Yacov Rambsel do that? How does he search the Bible codes without using a computer-software program? It seems too difficult or impossible to me!" Many people have asked Yacov these questions numerous times during the past several years. I had pondered that same question until one day I asked him to show me exactly how he does this. I was very impressed by how simple the procedure really is.

Here is how it works: Yacov chooses a certain scan of Hebrew Masoretic Text. For instance, he might choose to copy by hand all the letters in Hebrew of the entire first chapter of Genesis, which is the first book in the Torah, one of the Five Books of Moses. He carefully writes down each Hebrew letter of the text, each one directly under the previous one, leaving no spaces between words and sentences. This, of course, forms a vertical column of letters and is repeated a specified number of times, forming a matrix, a pattern of letters comprising ELS, which is the *Equidistant Letter Sequence.*

ELS codes are equally spaced letter-skips and are used to determine the location of the *key,* or *beginning, search code.* The total number of letter-skips can be anywhere from one on up, and going into many thousands. The search code can be the name of a person, place, or thing; it can also specify the name of an event. Most of the time, Yacov uses only *short* distances between letter-skips of the ELS codes. Logically, these short distances of ELS quickly help to identify and verify the key search code. Sometimes, it should be noted, Yacov includes information within some ELS codes that use plus (+) or minus (-) signs. The *plus* sign is used to locate an ELS code that is counted from right to left; the *minus* sign locates an ELS code that is counted from left to right.

Using the above system, Yacov researches and analyzes the Hebrew Scriptures for previously unknown encoded words and phrases related to a certain theme (the key search code). He has developed the amazing ability to simultaneously spot the correct combinations of words, phrases, and even complete sentences in certain cases.

By way of comparison to the scientific world, I refer the reader to a front-page article in the *USA Today* for June 23, 2000, which summarizes highlights of the completed Human Genome Project (publicly funded) and the Celera program (privately funded). For the past ten years, thousands of scientists world-wide have been "mapping" the genetic (DNA code) sequence, or "blueprint," of the human body. The data collected by researchers, according to this genetic "map," revealed that our DNA code, using a wide variety of sequences based on each gene's specialized function, expresses itself in "sentences" composed of 3.5 billion "letters." This genetic "blueprint" is also described as the Book of Life.

As news of this DNA-mapping began "running to and fro" throughout television, radio, the Internet, etc., this event was equated to the first moon landing. However, this "first genetic landing," as fascinating as it is, cannot begin to compare with the magnificently designed codes that God placed within His Book of Life, the Holy Bible's Hebrew text. He spoke His Word, instantly creating the universe, which follows the original pattern of His precious Word. It stands to reason that *all* things would be encrypted within *and* on the surface reading of the Holy Bible.

I believe, as many Bible scholars have in the past, that every person—from the poor and unknown to the rich and famous—is found somewhere within the Holy Bible. *Yes, even you and the circumstances in your life are encoded within the Hebrew text of the Holy Bible!*

Perhaps the following example will help you understand. Encoded in the book of Genesis is a very common name of a woman who may have lived in the past or is presently living now. In Genesis 17:19, starting with the first letter in the 11th word, counting forward every 34th letter spells *Sarah Smith;* שרה שמת. Because her name is encoded in the Bible does not mean she is famous or less fortunate. This insight will give you an idea of the massive information that is cryptically placed throughout the Holy Scriptures.

An additional insight may assist you in understanding the vast array of data God has placed within His Holy Word. These codes reveal *amazing truths that are being unveiled* for us by the

Holy Spirit in these last days. The insight that inspires me is the series of closely related codes that give a vivid description of the television ministry of TBN.

Genesis 7:13. Starting with the third letter in the eighth word and counting forward every 15th letter spells *Paul;* פלה. However, the Old Testament name of *Paul* is שאול, which is also encoded in the same area. Adjacent to his name at the same ELS is *Jan;* ין, which is the name of his wife.

But wait, there is much more that identifies Paul and Jan Crouch and their calling in this life.

Genesis 7:11. Starting with the fourth letter in the third word, counting forward every 20th letter spells *TBN;* תבן. Adjacent letters at the same ELS spell at least eleven different words that are directly associated with their work.

1. TBN
2. Paul
3. Jan
4. Crouch
5. Good News
6. Satellite
7. The photo image (TV)
8. Film
9. Praise
10. Shall be clothed with faith
11. Information; knowledge

The amazing fact is that all these words and phrases are at the same *equidistant letter sequence.* The statistical odds of this happening by chance are far beyond human capability.

Amazingly, some people still insist that there are no complete sentences within the Bible's Hebrew codes. However, this viewpoint does not change the fact that complete sentences *are* distributed throughout the Hebrew Masoretic Text, as you will see throughout this book.

Yaphrah Rambsel

March 21, 2000—14 Adar II, 5760

Feast of Purim

WHY SHOULD
I LEARN HEBREW?

Welcome to the exciting and unique adventure known as "the Bible codes" of Hebrew! Yes, it *is* an adventure, and as you continue reading and studying this book, you will be amazed at the extent of these codes and how they often reflect the surface, or plain, text of the Hebrew language of the Holy Scriptures.

Right now, you may be thinking: *Why should I care about what the Bible says on any subject—much less the so-called "Bible codes"? And why should I learn Hebrew? Isn't that a dead language, anyway? And isn't the Bible just a book full of myths or wishful thinking and rantings and ravings written by some mean old men who dared to call themselves "prophets"? And aren't their "prophecies" being used by some preachers trying to scare me into joining their church group, with the sole purpose of making me feel nervous while sitting in a fancy church pew (should I ever want to attend a church service)?*

Whew! Calmly now, consider some fascinating details about this beautiful language called Hebrew. First of all, Hebrew is written and read from *right to left.* Second, did you know that 80 percent of the root words of the English language can be traced back many thousands of years to biblical Hebrew? Consider what

William Tyndale (1492?—1536) said: "The English agreeth one thousand times more with the Hebrew than the Latin or the Greek." And not only is English overflowing with Hebraic origins, but there are hundreds of other languages and dialects enriched by Hebrew's influences.

Perhaps a few facts that I discovered in *THE WORD: The Dictionary That Reveals the Hebrew Sources of English* will show you the value of understanding Hebrew. In the ROOTS category (page 13), he tells us that "ABERRA(TION)/עבירה; AH-VEY-RAH is an abnormality; a transgression in Hebrew is an עבירה/ABHARA." Mozeson continues: "Latin words *ab* (from) and *errare* (to wander) form the etymology of ABERRATION."

In the *BRANCHES* category, "AVARA/עבירה brings us to AVOR/עבר, 'the root verb', which means to *over*step one's bounds by violating a norm or disobeying a rule. In Joshua 7:11 Israel 'transgressed' the covenant, while Mordecai the Jew in Esther 3:3 would not bend to Haman and 'disobeyed' the king's order.

"Why did Abraham cross Mesopotamia? To get to (or from) the Other Side." The reader is then referred to *other* listings in this book of "sound-alike words that 'cross-over' time and space." Some of these are: "FERRY; OVER; PARA(SITE); VEER." In *ROOTS* (page 72), under the entry "FERRY/הרבע; AH-VARA," "the Anglo-Saxon word for *ferry* is *ferian*, which means *to convey* or *carry*; Greek *pherein* means *to carry*." BRANCHES: "*Faru* in Anglo-Saxon is *a journey*; Arabic *(yous)afir* (travel) gave us SAFARI."

Hebrew/עברית/IVRIT (the language) is derived from the name of Eber/עבר, which means "colonizer." He was an ancestor of the Hebrew people and is first mentioned in Genesis 10:21.

So, why learn Hebrew? I believe you will gain a deeper appreciation for your native tongue, while learning the beauty and precision of Hebrew.

Finally, this writer would like to thank you, the reader, for allowing her *to carry* you in the *ferry-boat* of these words into the wonders of the Hebrew language. She hopes that she has brought you happily OVAR/עבר/OVER to the next page, so that you can get acquainted with the Hebrew Aleph-Beit [Alphabet].

Yaphah Rambsel

ACKNOWLEDGMENTS

I dedicate this book to everyone who loves the Word of God. I want to thank all my friends and relatives for their encouragement of my writing this volume concerning the Bible codes. I am especially grateful to my wife, Yaphah, for her dedication in co-writing and editing this volume. James and Alene Rambsel, our son and daughter, whom we love very much, have given us undying encouragement. I want to personally thank Dr. Paul Crouch, president of TBN, for his spiritual guidance and motivation for this writing. But most of all, I thank my God for endowing me with the spiritual strength in the research of His Holy Word.

Yacov Rambsel

One

THE GENESIS FACTOR

T he Holy Bible is a complete record of events—past, present, and future. Inspired by God Himself, it is a compilation of life-giving instructions to all mankind. This dynamic Book, as it reveals precious thoughts flowing from our Creator's heart and mind, describes in breathtaking detail the simplicities and the complexities of earth, our lives in general, as well as the universe. Its boundless information is for every class of people. No matter where you are living on earth, regardless of your vocational and educational background, I want you to know that there has never been—and never will be—another book like the Bible.

If you search through all the records of the writings in this world since the beginning of time, you will come to the startling conclusion that the Holy Bible is the only book that fulfills *all* its promises for spiritual and natural needs of every human being who has ever lived. The divine design of the Word of God is prophetically, historically, and textually *inerrant*. In other words, it is without error.

Now, that is a strong statement! However, the purpose of this book is to prove the validity of the Holy Bible's Scriptures beyond the shadow of a doubt by using a wide variety of examples from the fields of biblical archaeology, paleontology, astronomy, statistical analysis, and the mathematics of Bible codes research—equidistant letter sequence (ELS).

The Bible contains unlimited information about the creation, clearly described with statements from the surface, or plain, text, as well as hidden words, phrases, or statements, alluding to all the dispensations of time and the culmination of the ages. These prophetic events are set in stone and are unconditional prophecies that will come to pass, each one in its divine order and time.

Specifically, the first chapter of Genesis is written in such a way that it can be described as the chief cornerstone of *all* the Scriptures. Amazingly, it is densely packed with numerous, mind-boggling insights, guiding the reader through a panorama of the entire Holy Bible. The very first thing God created was *the time factor. In the beginning God created the heavens and the earth* (Genesis 1:1). Notice the phrase, *in the beginning.* This verse describes the beginning of the creation of the natural world and of time itself.

As the wonderful story in Genesis unfolds, God instructs Moses, one of His prophets, to write about some vital scientific truths, describing the perfect order of events as designed by the Creator. Letter by letter, God dictates to Moses, who writes it all down, telling us in clear language that the first six days of Creation and the seventh day for rest are equidistantly spaced at twenty-four hours for each day.

Not only are there ELS codes for letters and words, but also time periods that consist of a precisely designed, sequential order. The record of the first seven days is like a miniature picture in a time capsule, illustrating a monumental prophetic overview of God's plan of the ages. Days, weeks, months, years, jubilees, and millenniums are fulfilled, according to their designated perspectives and by God's divine timetable.

Your daily life is a sequence of common events, comprising every moment of your being—such as your eating and working habits and other activities of life in general. You set your clocks and watches to help establish and maintain control in your life, which is propelled by the regulation of time. For a moment or two, you break away from the daily sequence of your routine to enjoy a time of relaxation, but only to return to the daily, weekly, monthly, and yearly timetable. Regardless of what you are doing with your life, you are being monitored by the sequential heartbeat of your biological timeclock.

Solomon put it this way: *To every thing there is a season, and a time to every purpose under the heaven* (Ecclesiastes 3:1).

GENESIS CHAPTER ONE

The first chapter of Genesis is a magnificent matrix of insights, which are cryptologically structured words, phrases, and, sometimes, statements, reaching beyond time and space as we know it. There are also thousands of encoded words and phrases located within this same chapter, giving us natural and spiritual guidance. They reveal the divine pattern for the rest of the Holy Bible.

This foundational chapter of Genesis can be compared to an immense mine of deeply embedded jewels of revelation, each one representing a unique topic as well as interrelated ones. It should be prayerfully explored. It is like a never-ending roll call of names of people, cities, and events, which were written thousands of years before they (respectively) were born, were built, or happened. Nevertheless, the information derived from the surface reading of His Word, which a child can understand, is sufficient to guide us into a holy walk with the Lord.

In the following series of paragraphs is a sample of its encoded insights from Hebrew words, phrases, and sentences. Throughout this book, I develop similar paragraphs that set the standard for describing the details and results of my discoveries in the ELS codes.

Genesis 1:2. Starting with the fourth letter in the second word, counting forward every 66th letter spells *mountain of names; ha'shmoht;* הר־שמות. The adjacent letters at the same ELS spell *search out (examine); chahkar;* חקר.

Genesis 1:18. Starting with the fourth letter in the second word, counting in reverse every 40th letter spells *examine the dictionary; milon bur;* מילון בור. The adjacent letters at the same ELS spell *scrutinize the letters; ha'ohti shavar;* שבר האותי. This can also mean *to mark the letters.*

ASTRONOMY, GRAVITY, AND SIR ISAAC NEWTON

When God created the stars and the moon (Genesis 1:14-19), He also placed within this area of Scripture several encoded insights, naming some of the popular constellations in our vast universe, which are controlled by gravity. This information is very enlightening for astronomers as well as the average person.

Genesis 1:14-19. (14) *And God said, Let there be lights in the firmament of the heaven to divide the day from the night; and let them be for signs, and for seasons, and for days, and years: (15) And let them be for lights in the firmament of the heaven to give light upon the earth: and it was so. (16) And God made two great lights; the greater light to rule the day, and the lesser light to rule the night: he made the stars also. (17) And God set them in the firmament of the heaven to give light upon the earth, (18) And to rule over the day and over the night, and to divide the light from the darkness: and God saw that it was good. (19) And the evening and the morning were the fourth day.*

14 ויאמר אלהים יהי מארת ברקיע השמים להבדיל בין

היום ובין הלילה והיו לאתת ולמועדים ולימים ושנים:

15 והיו למארת ברקיע השמים להאיר על־הארץ ויהי־

כן: 16 ויעש אלהים את־שני המארת הגדלים את־המאור

הגדל לממשלת היום ואת־המאור הקטן לממשלת

הלילה ואת הכוכבים: 17 ויתן אתם אלהים ברקיע

השמים להאיר על־הארץ: 18 ולמשל ביום ובלילה

ולהבדיל בין האור ובין החשך וירא אלהים כי־טוב:

19 ויהי־ערב ויהי־בקר יום רביעי:

Genesis 1:14. Starting with the fifth letter in the fifth word, counting in reverse every 13th letter spells *Bear; aish;* עיש. The adjacent letters at the same ELS spell *Lion; ari'yah;* אריה.

Genesis 1:18. Starting with the first letter in the 11th word, counting in reverse every 54th letter spells *Pleiades; kimah;* כימה. This also means *the group of seven stars,* which is the Big Dipper.

Genesis 1:14. Starting with the first letter in the ninth word, counting forward every 19th letter spells *the South; ha'Taiman;* התימן. This word is used in Job 9:9. The adjacent letters to *ha'Taiman* spell *measuring line of codes; lekov kodi;* לקו קודי.

From these verses we gain the following insights. The plus sign (+) indicates an ELS code that is counted from right to left. The minus sign (-) indicates that it is counted from left to right.

1. The Bear (Arcturus) -13.

2. The Lion (Leo) -13.

3. Pleiades (Big Dipper) -54.

4. The South (Ha'Taiman) + 19.

5. Measuring line of codes + 19.

As a special note, the Yiddish name for *Leo the Lion; lebal;* לבל is also encoded in this same area of Scripture.

Job 9:9. ...*who made the Bear, Orion, Pleiades, and the chambers of the south [Ha'Taiman]* תימן [Interlinear Hebrew Bible].

עשה שע כסיל וכימה וחדרי תימן:

God had revealed to Job the wonderful information about the various constellations in our universe and called them by name. Without a doubt, this proves that the Word of God is of divine origin, and that God is the Designer and Finisher of His own creation.

Habakkuk 3:3. *God comes from Teman* [תימן], *and the Holy One from Mount Paran. Selah. His Majesty covers the heavens, and His praise fills the earth* [Interlinear Hebrew Bible].

Teman is in the southern part of the universe, as determined from the earthly point of calculation. Somewhere in the ageless realm of an invisible universe, God makes His abode. However, God is a Spirit and dwells in a non-material realm beyond our physical, four-dimensional plane. But He fills all of His creation, even our earthly dwelling. As a matter of fact, the whole universe is in Him.

The world in which we live is the house of natural and spiritual light that God made for us. It is His gift to all generations—past, present, and future—throughout the ceaseless ages to come. However, the universe is like one enormously vast house full of light that shines from one end to the other. Stars, solar systems, and galaxies of all sizes are set in place just waiting for our discovery and exploration. God created the sun and unimaginable billions of stars throughout the universe. He also controls the speed of light, which travels at 186,000 miles per second. Since the Lord is the Father of all lights—spiritual or natural—all light emanates from Him.

Two of the major elements that were present when God created the heavens and the earth were His Light and His Word. His words are life and eternal, and His Spirit is pure Light, abounding with ultimate power. He is our God, the Father of life. The six days of creation are recorded in the first chapter of Genesis. However, there are other portions of the Bible that give additional, detailed information concerning God's creation.

There are 434 Hebrew words with a total of 1,671 letters comprising this first chapter, which contains references to the past, present, and future ages. It is like a gigantic, heavenly information center, describing many intriguing names of people, places, and events on this earth and the whole universe. Who, but God, could have known in advance the existence of every person who would ever be born into this world—not only their names, but the events in their lives as well?

The power that controls gravity is the Word of God. When God created the celestial bodies, He also placed the law of gravity in motion. There are some interesting insights in regard to the man who discovered and revealed the laws of gravity to the whole world.

Sir Isaac Newton was a brilliant scientist and is considered by many mathematicians to be the father of calculus. This was not his only achievement, but it seems to be at the top of the list for most researchers in this field.

Genesis 1:9. Starting with the fourth letter in the eighth word, counting forward every 222nd letter spells *gravity;*

m'shikah; משיכה. This is the force that rules the movements of all things throughout the universe, including our ocean tides on earth. In Numbers 18:7, the name Newton is encoded. Crossing his name at six-ELS is the Hebrew word for *gravity; ha'mishikah;* המשיכה.

SPEED OF LIGHT AND CIRCLES

At the dawn of creation as recorded in Genesis 1:2, there is an encoded phrase at six-letter intervals that spells *lighthouse; bait a'or;* בית אור. However, this phrase is encoded again in the area of Scripture telling us when God created the sun, stars, and planets.

Genesis 1:17. Starting with the first letter in the fourth word, counting in reverse every 94th letter spells *lighthouse;* אור בית. The adjacent letters at the same sequence spell *speed conceived; mohar harah;* מהר הרה. The first insight refers to the spiritual lighthouse, and the second, the natural lighthouse and the speed at which light travels.

In this same area of Scripture the ineffable name of *Jehovah Adonai aleph;* יהוה א is encoded. When spelled out in three letters, *aleph;* אלף means 1,000. There is a simple equation that is used to calculate the speed of light when multiplying His name by 1,000. Since all light radiates from Him, it would stand to reason that within His name, there resides the essence (sum and substance) of a pure and brilliant light, confirming what the astronomers have already discovered.

The name of *Jehovah* in Hebrew is יהוה, and the combination of the four letters add up to a grand total of twenty-six (26).

The *yod* (י) is   10
The *heh* (ה) is   5
The *vav* (ו) is   6
The *heh* (ה) is   5
              26

When each letter above, independently, is taken to the second power, then added together, that total value is 186^2.

The *yod* (י) to the second power equals   100
The *heh* (ה) to the second power equals   25
The *vav* (ו) to the second power equals   36
The *heh* (ה) to the second power equals   25
              186

Multiply יהוה (186) by אלף (1,000), and the result is 186,000, which is the speed of light. The *aleph;* אלף, when spelled out in its three-letter combination also has a numerical value of 111, which is the same as the Hebrew word for *circumference; kavah;* קוה or *measuring line.*

The speed of light is used by scientists as a measuring device for gauging the vast distances of other planets and star systems. Since light is the fastest moving substance known to natural man, it is the only standard available to him.

Genesis 1:19. Starting with the third letter in the first word, counting forward every fifth letter spells *measuring line of light; a'or kavah;* אור קוה. Another way to say this is *light the measuring line.*

Genesis 1:5. Starting with the first letter in the sixth word, counting in reverse every tenth letter spells *kav kavah*; קן קוה; *circumference line.* The *line; kav;* קן equals 106 and *the circumference;* קוה equals 111. The formula, 3 x 111 ÷ 106 = *pi*; 3.1415.

Another way of saying this is *the diameter of a circle times pi (3.1415) equals the circumference.* In geometry the ratio between diameter and circumference is *pi* (3.1415). *The circle itself is a picture of infinity—no beginning and no ending.* This fascinating insight gives us some very unusual information, which reveals the precision of the mathematical structure of His Word and the whole universe.

Aided by the magnificent Hubble telescope and the rapid advancement in many fields of science, I believe we are on the leading edge of the final truth of the whole universe and its contents.

ELS CODES AND PROPHETICAL TIMETABLES

The simple illustration below, describing the second day of Creation, is taken from the Hebrew Masoretic Text. It will give you a clear idea of how the ELS codes are placed throughout the Scriptures.

Genesis 1:6-8. (6) *And God said, Let there be a firmament in the midst of the waters, and let it divide the waters from the waters. (7) And God made the firmament, and divided the waters which were under the firmament from the waters which were above the firmament: and it was so. (8) And God called the firmament Heaven. And the evening and the morning were the second day.*

6 ויאמר אלהים יהי רקיע בתוך המים ויהי מבדיל בין
מים למים: 7 ויעש אלהים את־הרקיע ויבדל בין המים
אשר מתחת לרקיע ובין המים אשר מעל לרקיע ויהי־כן:
ויקרא אלהים לרקיע שמים ויהי־ערב ויהי־בקר יום שני:

Genesis 1:7. Starting with the second letter in the 13th word, counting in reverse every 14th letter spells *equidistant sequences; shahlavim;* שלבים.

The true meaning of this word from the biblical Hebrew is *equally spaced intervals*, but from the modern Hebrew it means *equally spaced rungs on a ladder*. Either rendition conveys the same and proper meaning. However, the *meaning* of this insight is *the exact method I used to locate this code.*

The following insight is at very low intervals, thus reinforcing the above code.

Genesis 1:7. Starting with the third letter in the fourth word, counting forward every third letter spells *the codes of truth; kod'dim emet;* קודים אמת, which also translates as *hidden truths.* Another Hebrew word for code or *something hidden* is *tzophen;* צופן. Both of these words are encoded (hidden) in the first chapter of Genesis.

A mathematical analysis in the first chapter of Genesis was performed on the Hebrew phrase *the codes of truth*. The odds of this phrase happening by chance are less than *.00002 to one million* or more than 10 billion to one.

Two of the methods God uses to convey a prophetic message to us is by a direct prophecy or a Scripture that alludes to a greater truth. The following insights give us a clearer under-standing of God's methodology, which is demonstrated in His written Word as forever settled in heaven.

Genesis 1:8. Starting with the second letter in the fourth word, counting in reverse every 29th letter spells *teleologically motivated; me'anim;* מעניס. This word also means *the purpose of an event that refers to the future* or *a prophetic parable.* Oddly enough, the encoded phrase adjacent to the above insight at the same sequence gives us more information concerning the prophetic parable, which is *to prolong (stretch out) the division;* שרע הבדל. This could refer to *the prophetic timetable of the com-pletion of all things.*

DNA AND MANKIND

When God created the animals on the sixth day, He also created man on the same day. When God made Adam from the dust of the earth, He did not make him a baby, but a fully grown man. If you had asked Adam how old he was, his response would have been simple and direct: *"I am but a few hours old."* Yet you would not have seen an embryo or fetus, but a mature man made in the image of God. The Creator of all things demonstrated His creative genius by overlapping the normal time sequence for growth. In other words, the Lord condensed time and created Adam into full stature.

Think for a moment about what took place when God cre-ated the thousands of various species of animals on the fifth and sixth days, respectively. Then consider Genesis 2:23, describing how God took a rib from Adam and formed the woman, who also was fully grown and completely mature. Her DNA, created by and a gift from God Himself, was taken from man.

In the record of the creation of man, the letters for DNA are encoded twice—one at five-letter intervals and the other at six-letter intervals. This is found in Genesis 1:26. Perhaps the six-letter intervals represent the day when Adam was created as well as the number of man being represented by the number six.

God gave us a greater demonstration of His creative faculties when He created man in His own image. The Lord not only gave man a body, soul, and a spirit, but He put in man a spark of life that comes from God Himself. Adam knew God as his Father when he saw Him for the first time. There was a harmonious relationship between the created man and his Creator.

The area of Scripture that describes the creation of man gives us some delightful information concerning God's goal for mankind in general.

Genesis 1:26-27. (26) *And God said, Let Us make man in Our image, according to Our likeness; and let them rule over the fish of the sea, and over the birds of the heavens, and over the cattle, and over all the earth, and over all the creepers creeping on the earth. (27) And God created the man in His own image; in the image of God He created him. He created them male and female.* [Interlinear Hebrew Bible]

26 ויאמר אלהים נעשׂה אדם בצלמנו כדמותנו וירדו

בדגת הים ובעוף השמים ובבהמה ובכל־הארץ ובכל־

הרמש הרמש על־הארץ: 27 ויברא אלהים את־האדם
בצלמו בצלם אלהים ברא אתו זכר ונקבה ברא אתם:

Genesis 1:26. Starting with the first letter in the 17th word, counting in reverse every 17th letter spells *the Temple; ha'hai'kal*, ההיכל.

There are several other insights that are encoded at 17-letter increments in this same Hebrew text, revealing additional information concerning the man that God created. Adam was created as an innocent adult with faculties that far surpass our capabilities today. Adam was also a type of the completed man and in full stature—spiritually, mentally, and physically.

With the first man, God had put in motion His plan of redemption for all His creation. This magnificent and heavenly plan preempted the fall in the garden of Eden, when Adam and Eve ate of the forbidden fruit. The creation of the universe and mankind was a type of embryo that grows into its full maturity. In God's time we shall awake in His likeness, shrouded with His beauty and resplendent nature.

There are five very descriptive and precise words and phrases that are encoded in these two verses, all at 17-letter increments.

1. Jehovah; יהוה.

2. The Temple; ההיכל.

3. Man preserved; איש מלט.

4. In the light; באור.

5. Created; ברא.

Man is the temple of the Lord God and His light dwells within us. He will preserve us if we walk in the light as He is in the light, *for in His light we shall see more light.*

There are many dimensions to God's creation, both natural and spiritual. However, because we live in a four-dimensional world, it is generally beyond our intellectual capabilities to comprehend anything but height, width, depth, and time. It is said by some scientists that the universe expands into the 11th dimension, which is far beyond human understanding. When I meditate on the depth, height, and width of God, I can only give adoration to Him by the faculties with which He has endowed me.

He has created my *eyes* that I may see His glory; my *ears* that I may hear His voice; my *nose* that I may sense His heavenly aroma; my *mouth* that I may sing praises, give testimony unto Him, and taste to see that the Lord is good; my *hands* that I may do service unto Him and raise my hands in praise to Him; my *feet* that I may walk in His ways; my *legs* that I may run this holy race, and my *heart* that I may love Him and the unlovable from the inner sanctum of my being. Yes, we are created in the image of God to grow in His likeness now and forevermore. We are still in the embryo stage, but one day soon we shall behold Him and see Him as He is. Then we shall know Him as we are known of Him.

DINOSAURS, MAN, AND THE FLOOD

The overwhelming scientific evidence that man and dinosaurs coexisted refutes the secular teaching that the dinosaurs became extinct many millions of year ago. As a matter of fact, the evidence discovered by some leading archeologists around the world have presented undeniable proof that man and dinosaurs lived on earth at the same time, and as recently as four or five thousand years ago.

Of all the animals that God created, none are as fascinating as the dinosaurs. The majestic stature of these magnificent beasts surpasses all the others in the animal kingdom. The debate still goes on: *How and when did the dinosaurs disappear?*

From a biblical point of view, there is absolutely no argument. Men and dinosaurs lived together before the great flood of Noah's time. As a matter of fact, God instructed Noah to bring into the ark of refuge both male and female of all the animals from God's creation.

Dr. Carl Baugh, an archeologist, has written several books and provided sufficient evidence that man and dinosaurs coexisted. He says, "The evidence is conclusive. These dinosaurs were around much later than the critics allowed. And as they were on a stratum ABOVE human footprints (as well as on the SAME stratum as other dinosaur and human footprints), dinosaurs and humans were indeed contemporary."[1]

Dr. Baugh's books actually have photographs that provide even further evidence to examine. The following description shows the photographed footprints in detail.

---

[1] Carl E. Baugh and Clifford Wilson, *Footprints and the Stones of Time* (Oklahoma City: Hearthstone Publishing, Inc., 1994), p. 103.

By 1992 erosion revealed that this footprint was directly beside the 134 dinosaur prints on the same platform. The entire trail of human-like tracks is among, within, across and, in this case, *beside* 25" dinosaur tracks. The cast of a fossil footprint was made by Stan Taylor in 1970.

The lower left picture of the same print, taken in 1988, shows the effect of 18 years of erosion. A chunk came out of the left side, but the same general shape can be seen.

On August 12, 1989, geologist Don Patton spoke at a creation conference in Dayton, Tennessee. He presented evidence that all the data relating to the Taylor Trail was best explained by a combination of human and dinosaur tracks....The fossil footprint seen in these pictures is called the Ryals Track, named for Jim Ryals, who removed a beautiful left footprint from the Paluxy River bed, back in the '30s. The resulting hole in the Cretaceous limestone can be seen directly ahead of this right footprint. The track Ryals removed was on display for years in the courtyard of Dr. Cook's medical clinic in Cleburne, Texas.

The toes of this track extend back under an overhang formed when the foot was pulled out of the calcareous "mud." The same feature can be seen in some of the hundreds of dinosaur tracks found in the same layer. When the individual stepped forward, the toes drug, leaving impressions in the now hard limestone."[2]

Interestingly, this seems to indicate that the people and the animals had been running in the same direction, as though they had been fleeing from something that was rapidly approaching. Could it have been the flood of Noah's day?

In July of 1997, my wife Yaphah and I visited Dr. Carl Baugh's Creation Evidences Museum in Glen Rose, Texas. We were thrilled to see the evidence of a human footprint overlapped by a dinosaur's print. This proves that the account in Genesis is true and that the flood of Noah's time did actually take place as the Bible describes it. On display at the Creation Evidences Museum are Dr. Baugh's many collections of fossilized prints of humans and dinosaurs, some of which give evidence of a great flood.

To my amazement, I found encoded in the first chapter of Genesis man and the dinosaur together. It contains at least three dynamic codes that parallel the archeological findings of our day, concerning man and the so-called prehistoric dinosaurs. The evidence presented thus far is from a logical and scientific point of view.

Genesis 1:21. Starting with the first letter in the tenth word, counting in reverse every 144th letter spells *the dinosaurs; ha'behimmoti;* הבהמותי. The adjacent letters also at 144-ELS spell *man; Adahm;* אדם.

---

[2]Baugh, Dr. Carl, *Why Do Men Believe Evolution Against All Odds?* (Oklahoma City: Hearthstone Publishing, Inc., 1999), pp. 101-103.

A recent statistical analysis was made on the probabilities of these insights occurring by chance. The amazingly profound mathematical odds are .00005 to a million, or less than ten billion to one. This is another strong example that these insights were not placed in the Scriptures by chance.

I also found a third insight that adds future proof of the inerrant Word of God. I continued my analysis at 144-ELS and found the phrase, *from Job; me'aiyob;* מאיוב. This gave me an indication that there was additional information in the book of Job. In order to understand the significance of this code, I searched the section of Job where the same word is found in the surface reading.

Job 40:15-18. (15) *Behold now behemoth* [בהמות]*, which I made with thee; he eateth grass as an ox.* (16) *Lo now, his strength is in his loins, and his force is in the navel of his belly.* (17) *He moveth his tail like a cedar: the sinews of his stones are wrapped together.* (18) *His bones are as strong pieces of brass; his bones are like bars of iron.*

Did you notice the first thing God told Job? *I made the behemoth (dinosaur) with you (man).* This means that man and dinosaurs coexisted. This statement agrees with the sixth day of creation when the animals were created, then man.

The second thing God said was that this animal was very large and a vegetarian: *he eats grass as an ox.* Some translations interpret the behemoth as an ox or something similar. But the description given in Job is not that of an ox. Also, the overwhelming evidence found by today's leading paleontologists and archeologists proves that most dinosaurs were *not carnivorous.*

The third statement made was that *his tail was long and like a cedar tree.* The brontosaurus and the tyrannosaurus rex had tails like the cedar tree. These three elements in the above Scripture give us the description of the dinosaur, emphasizing the fact that these creatures existed in the time of Job.

The flood of Noah's day was caused by the rebellion of man toward God. The Creator could no longer wink at the evil that prevailed upon earth. God sent judgment in the form of the great flood, but Noah and his family were spared. God told Noah to build an ark [תבה] so that he and his three sons with their wives could survive the wrath of God that soon was going to be unleashed on the world. In Genesis 1:21, where it refers to the seas, there are combinations of encoded words that refer to *the flood, Noah, Ham, Shem, Japhet,* and *the ark.*

Genesis 1:21-23. (21) *And God created great whales, and every living creature that moveth, which the waters brought forth abundantly, after their kind, and every winged fowl after his kind: and God saw that it was good. (22) And God blessed them, saying, Be fruitful, and multiply, and fill the waters in the seas, and let fowl multiply in the earth. (23) And the evening and the morning were the fifth day.*

21 ויברא אלהים את־התנינם הגדלים ואת כל־נפש החיה הרמשת אשר
שרצו המים למינהם ואת כל־עוף כנף למינהו וירא אלהים כי־טוב:

22 ויברך אתם אלהים לאמר פרו ורבו ומלאו את־המים

בימים והעוף ירב בארץ: 23 ויהי־ערב ויהי־בקר יום חמישי:

Genesis 1:21. *Noah;* נח, *Shem;* שם, and *Yaphet;* יפת are all encoded at four-letter intervals, but *Ham;* חם is at five-letter intervals.

Genesis 1:22. Starting with the fifth letter in the third word, counting in reverse every 13th letter spells *(the) flood; mebul;* מבול. The adjacent letters at the same count spell *curse; arar;* ארר.

Genesis 1:22. Starting with the second letter in the second word, counting in reverse every seventh letter spells *Ark; Tavah;* תבה. It is interesting to note that this count is seven. It was on the seventh day, after Noah, his family, and the animals were in the ark, that the fountains of the deep gushed forth, the heavens broke up, and it rained for the very first time in history. As a matter of fact, it was a worldwide deluge for forty days and forty nights. None were spared, except those who were in the ark of safety. God created a perfect universe, but sin caused that which was perfect to become imperfect.

THE PERFECT CREATION

The number *seven* (7) and its multiples play an important role in the Creation. Seven has unique meanings, such as *fullness; completion; perfection.* There are seven words and 28 (4 x 7) letters that form the first verse in the Hebrew text. The 434 words of chapter one equal 7 x 62.

Genesis 1:1. Starting with the third letter in the third word, counting forward every 14th (2 x 7) letter spells *the sign; ha'oht;* האות. The phrase, *the sign,* means that God gave us a sign or information within the text, proving that He is the designer.

Genesis 1:1. Starting with the first letter in the fifth word, counting forward every 14th letter spells *the light; ha'a'or;* האור. This tells us that God sent forth the light that was present on day one.

Genesis 1:2. Starting with the third letter in the tenth word, counting forward every 14th letter spells *the speed (great rapidity); ha'mohairai;* המהרי. This data gives us additional information concerning the speed by which God sent forth His divine light.

The Hebrew phrase, *and God saw; va'yarai;* וירא אלהים, appears seven times in the first six days of creation. In other words, God looked at His creation seven times and saw that it was good and complete. Also, the Hebrew for *good; tov;* שוב appears seven times in the first six days of creation.

The Hebrew phrase, *Jehovah fathered; yoav;* יואב, is encoded at seven-letter increments in Genesis 2:2, where it states that God rested from His creative works. Adjacent letters, also at the same ELS, spell *Israel; Yisrael;* ישראל. I will develop this subject more in chapter seven.

There is an encoded phrase in Genesis 1:3-4, giving an insight describing the character and splendor of the Creator.

Genesis 1:3. Starting with the third letter in the fifth word, counting forward every fourth letter spells *the glory of Yah seen* *(revealed); ha're'ah'yah ha'kavod;* כברה הראיה. The Lord God saw that His resplendent glory filled the earth and it was good.

Genesis 1:3-4. (3) *And God said, Let there be light: and there was light.* (4) *And God saw the light, that it was good: and God divided the light from the darkness.*

3 ויאמר אלהים יהי אור ויהי־אור: וירא אלהים

4 את־האור כי־טוב ויבדל אלהים בין האור ובין החשׁך:

In Genesis 1:4, we find the Hebrew phrase, *the light; et ha'a'or;* את־האור, that gives us additional information of the glorious and holy character of our Lord God.

Each letter in the Hebrew text has a mathematical value (as stated before). When analyzing a word or phrase, according to the Hebrew way of calculating, very often we can receive a better understanding of the message that God is conveying to us.

The *aleph* [א] equals one (1); *tav* [ת] equals four hundred (400); *heh* [ה] equals five (5); *aleph* [א] equals one (1); *vav* [ו] equals six (6); *resh* [ר] equals two hundred (200). These letters added together equal 613.

It is amazing that 613 equals the total amount of commandments in the Torah, the five books of Moses, which reveal to us the absolute holiness of the Lord God. For without holiness, we cannot see God. This wonderful light that moved upon the face of the deep before the sun and the stars were created had to be the glorious light of His presence, which is His Holy Spirit.

The book of Wisdom, which is called Proverbs, opens our understanding of the importance of the laws of God. They are a lamp, light, and a way of life. *For the commandment is a lamp; and the law* [תורה] *is light; and reproofs of instruction are the way of life* (Proverbs 6:23).

God gave Israel certain commandments that had to be obeyed. The reason for this is that through Israel would come the Savior and Redeemer of the world. It is not impossible for anyone to keep these 613 laws, but God in His mercy has a redemptive plan for all who fall short of His holiness.

The Hebrew phrase, *the Lord God of Israel; Adonai Elohai Yisrael;* יהוה אלהי ישראל, also has a value of 613. Yet again, an encoded, previously hidden, insight opens up our understanding to the revelation that God is holy and emphasizes that these commandments are a reflection of that holiness.

When Moses was commanded by God to ascend Mount Sinai, the Lord told him to write every commandment and teach them to the whole house of Israel. The Hebrew phrase, *Moses our teacher; Moshe ravinu;* משה רבינו, also has a mathematical value of 613, which is the total amount of commandments he was instructed to teach. The Torah, the first five books of the Bible, are historic, instructional, and prophetic in nature. The complete Torah will be fulfilled by the Messiah of God, the Anointed One, within the proper time element as prescribed by the Lord God of Israel.

THE NATURAL ELEMENTS OF THE EARTH

Many of the earth's metals, such as gold, coal, carbon, zinc, copper, iron, tin, lead, nickel, chromium, uranium, and many more, are encoded within this chapter. It also gives many of the elements and compounds, such as oxygen, hydrogen, ether, helium, iodine, hydrogen-peroxide, and *the atom; ha'ahtohm;* האטום.

The word *hydrogen* and the phrase, *the basic principle*, are encoded adjacent to each other at the same ELS.

Genesis 1:9. Starting with the fourth letter in the eighth word, counting every 31st letter in reverse spells *hydrogen; maiman;* מימן. In Genesis 1:7, starting with the fifth letter in the fourth word, counting forward every 31st letter spells *basis (basic principle); aikar;* עיקר.

Note how that message compares to *The World Book Encyclopedia's* definition of hydrogen. "Hydrogen is a tasteless, odorless, colorless gas. It is the lightest element known. Hydrogen is of great importance to man, for it is found in water, in plant and animal tissues, in wood, paper, starch, fats, petroleum products, and almost every organic compound. It is also found in all acids and in many other chemical substances. Free or uncombined hydrogen is found chiefly in natural gases. Some authorities believe that the extreme upper portions of the air may be largely hydrogen. There are enormous amounts of hydrogen in the sun's atmosphere."

I would also note hydrogen peroxide, according to *Webster's Dictionary*, is an unstable compound, H_2O_2, a colorless, syrupy liquid, often used in dilute solution as a bleaching or disinfecting agent, and in more concentrated form as a rocket fuel, in the production of foam rubber, etc.

Amazingly, hydrogen shows up twice and oxygen once with the same minute ELS. This gives us the formula for *water* (H_2O) as is found in the first portion of Genesis. Moses, the author of the Torah, had no way of knowing the chemical composition of water, but God did (and does), proving that He had complete control over the writing of the Holy Bible. Hydrogen peroxide was not used in Biblical times, but the fact that the insight referring to it is encoded should give us an idea of how many insights project into the future.

Two

THE FOREKNOWLEDGE OF GOD

The crowning achievement of God in the first six days was the creation of a mature man. This should answer the question: Which came first—the chicken or the egg? Adam was created fully grown with God-given life, intelligence, and perfect health. One thing that placed Adam above the rest of the creation is that God breathed into him the breath of life and gave him a spirit. He was complete with a body, soul, and spirit.

A display of this God-like intellect was demonstrated when Adam named all the various animals. The very meaning of each animal's name was the precise description of a set of unique functions or characteristics of that creature. For example, he named the *bird oph;* עוֹף, because *oph* means *to cover with wings; to fly.*

There are thousands of encoded names of biblical characters in the first chapter of Genesis. Also, there are many encoded names of nations and places, each of which has the same name today as in ancient times. All the Hebrew months of the year and the feasts are encoded within the first two chapters of Genesis.

Frequently, modern names of people and places show up in the most unexpected places throughout the Hebrew text. Essentially, all these names have a special meaning or they would not have been encoded within the Bible. My purpose in this chapter, though, is to discuss the genealogy from Adam, David, and leading up to the Messiah as encoded within the first and second chapters of Genesis.

THE CREATION OF MAN IN THE IMAGE OF GOD

Genesis 1:25-27. (25) *And God made the beast of the earth after his kind, and cattle after their kind, and every thing that creepeth upon the earth after his kind: and God saw that it was good. (26) And God said, Let us make man in our image, after our likeness: and let them have dominion over the fish of the sea, and over the fowl of the air, and over the cattle, and over all the earth, and over every creeping thing that creepeth upon the earth. (27) So God created man in his own image, in the image of God created he him; male and female created he them.*

25 ויעש אלהים את־חית הארץ למינה ואת־הבהמה למינה

ואת כל־רמש האדמה למינהו וירא אלהים כי־טוב:

26 ויאמר אלהים נעשה אדם בצלמנו כדמותנו וירדו בדגת הים

ובעוף השמים ובבהמה ובכל־הארץ ובכל־הרמש הרמש

על־הארץ: 27 ויברא אלהים את־האדם בצלמו בצלם

אלהים ברא אתו זכר ונקבה ברא אתם:

There are two outstanding points to draw from these verses. First, that God created each animal after its own kind; therefore, each species brings forth of its own kind with uniquely inherited instincts. However, because God created man in His own image, this indicates that man has a higher goal in the ultimate course of events. The ultimate goal of man is to be free from sin and to be shrouded with God's heavenly nature and the grandeur of His presence.

There are encoded statements in the above Scriptures that reflect man's God-given intellect.

Genesis 1:24. Starting with the second letter in the seventh word, counting in reverse every 40th letter spells *the circumference of intelligent life; hakavah chaii he'shekalim;* הקוה חיי השכלים. The adjacent phrase with the same ELS spells *it will firmly be of uprightness in God; ahkain ye'hi yishri'el;* אכן היה ישריאל.

Notice that within the phrase, *uprightness in God,* is the nation of Israel; ישראל, which is a prophetic code referring to a nation that will be used for the glory of God. The circumference of a circle has no end; and so it was with Adam when God created him to live forever. But when sin entered into man's life, he would die physically and spiritually. However, the spirit and soul of man will never die regardless of the condition.

God knew Adam had no mate for companionship and for reproduction, but He wanted Adam to realize this fact. Therefore, the Lord God put in motion a segment of His redemptive plan of the ages to bring forth complete salvation for all people in every generation.

Genesis 2:19. *And out of the ground the LORD God formed every beast of the field, and every fowl of the air; and brought them* *unto Adam to see what he would call them: and whatsoever Adam called every living creature, that was the name thereof.*

God presented Adam with all the animals and an opportunity to have a part in the identification of all the creatures that God created. Therefore, when Adam completed the naming of all the animals and their mates, he was quite aware that he had no mate for himself. The man could not find any creature that was suited for himself. I am sure he thought that since the animals could reproduce, but that he could not, it was because he had no mate of the opposite sex from his own species.

God in His wisdom caused a deep sleep to come upon Adam. The word used is *tar'demah;* תרדמה, which alludes to a type of death. This was the method God used to bring forth a perfect bride.

Genesis 2:21-22. (21) *And the LORD God caused a deep sleep to fall upon Adam, and he slept: and he took one of his ribs, and closed up the flesh instead thereof;* (22) *And the rib, which the LORD God had taken from man, made he a woman, and brought her unto the man.*

After the surgery, God fused Adam's side and healed his wound. This was the very first operation in the history of mankind, involving the shedding of blood. The purpose of this event was to give Adam a loving mate and to populate the earth with his own kind. When God awakened the man from his sleep, he was presented with a magnificently beautiful woman—fully grown and mature. Adam called her *Aishah;* אשה, which means *Wo'man,* because she came forth from *Aish;* איש; *Man.*

According to the ancient Hebrew scholars, the name *Adam;* אדם has a genealogical and prophetic significance. The (*a*) represents Adam, the (*d*) David, and (*m*) the Messiah. They believed and taught that God's Messiah would come through the royal blood line of Adam and David and his descendants.

Most beautiful is the Word of God. Our Lord placed within the confines of this area of Scripture the name David and the Messiah. Both names come from the same word, *deep sleep;* תרדמה.

Genesis 2:21. Starting with the fourth letter in the fourth word, counting in reverse every 49th letter spells *Messiah; Mashiach;* משיח. From the same word David shows up at 47-ELS.

The Hebrew word that God used for *deep sleep* in this text has within it two words that have two related meanings. The first two letters mean *tor;* תר, which means *the turtle dove.* The turtle dove was an innocent bird that was used in a sacrificial offering unto the Lord. The next two letters are *dahm;* דם, which means *blood.* These two combinations in the same word refer to the innocent Man who would shed His blood for a bride. This is exactly what Adam did. Since Adam was a type of the Messiah, this alludes to a far greater event to be fulfilled in the future.

THE FALL

Adam and his wife lived in the Garden of Eden. The Lord had told the man not to eat of the tree of knowledge of good and evil. However, *the serpent;* הנחש tempted the woman, who ate of it; then she gave some to her husband so that he partook of this forbidden fruit. The scene that follows is too horrible to describe.

God told Adam that in the day when he ate the fruit from the tree of the knowledge of good and evil, he would die. This death would take place within his body, soul, and spirit. When they ate of this fruit, a reversed transformation took place. They both died in their bodies, souls, and spirits because they disobeyed the commandment of God. When mankind's total redemption would take place in a far-distant future, it must be for the whole body, soul, and spirit; otherwise, it would be incomplete.

However, Adam lived 930 years (Genesis 5:5). How could this be, since he lived longer than a twenty-four-hour day after his partaking of the forbidden fruit? This is the first appearance in the Bible indicating that the day to which God was referring is "as a thousand years." The first man lived 93 percent of a day (one thousand years), and he died. However, Methuselah lived longer—96.9 percent of a day—than any other human on the face of the earth.

There is an amazing encoded insight reflecting the above Scripture in the area of the first chapter of Genesis when God created the animals and man.

Genesis 1:24. Starting with the third letter in the first word, counting forward every 930 letters spells *Adam;* אדם. The adjacent letters at the same ELS spell *Eve,* חוה; *Cain,* קין; *Abel,* הבל; and Abel's replacement, *Seth;* שת. When counting each letter as a year, this gives us the years that Adam lived. However, there is no record in God's Word hinting at the age of Eve when she died. It is not unusual for Adam to show up at this count, since his name has only three Hebrew letters, but for Eve and their three sons to appear at the same sequence is quite another thing.

The phenomena of these codes alone are enough to cause the skeptic to wonder if there is something to it after all. But for those who already believe that the Bible is God's Word, it increases their faith in the written word and their Creator.

THE COMING REDEMPTION

After sin entered Adam and Eve, they feared God from that day forward. On one occasion, when they heard God walking in the garden and conversing with them as was His daily custom, they immediately made coverings for themselves with fig leaves. As the conversation continued, Adam blamed Eve, but God knew that both of them were guilty of disobedience.

The all-knowing and all-loving Lord God was aware that the covering that Adam and Eve had made for themselves would not be sufficient to cover their shame. So God in His mercy sacrificed an innocent animal, perhaps a lamb, and took the hide and covered the man and the woman. For the redemption process to be complete, it must be completed by God—not man. This is the second time in the Bible that innocent blood was shed. Analyzing this event, we see another picture of the redemptive plan of God in action.

God pronounced judgment on the serpent that tempted Eve, and at the same time gave a promise to the man and the woman that her seed one day would crush the head of the serpent and eradicate his influence upon the human race. This was the first direct mention of the Messiah who would come through Adam and Eve and the following generations for their complete deliverance from the curse of death.

Genesis 3:15. *And I will put enmity between thee and the woman, and between thy seed and her seed; it [He] shall bruise thy head, and thou shalt bruise his heel.* The phrase, *shalt bruise his heel,* refers to the coming Messiah and the nation that would bring forth the Anointed One from God. The serpent (Satan) would persecute that nation until the Deliverer would come. But if that nation as a whole would not receive the Messiah when He came, they would be rejected in measure until the time of the restoration of all things, which would take place during the era of *the Messianic kingdom.*

The phrase, *the seed of the woman,* could be misinterpreted because a woman does not have seed; the man does instead. When we look at another prophecy referring to a virgin who will conceive, we can better understand what the phrase, *seed of the woman,* means. For a virgin to conceive an embryo, a heavenly miracle must take place; the seed must be produced by the Holy Spirit of God, because *only* God can create life.

Isaiah 7:13-14. (13) *And he said, Hear ye now, O house of David; Is it a small thing for you to weary men, but will ye weary* *my God also? (14) Therefore the Lord himself shall give you a sign; Behold, a virgin shall conceive, and bear a son, and shall call his name Immanuel.*

There are four important facts about this Scripture to consider.

1. The Lord will give a sign.

2. A virgin shall conceive.

3. A son shall be born.

4. His name is Immanuel (God with us).

When we consider the implications involved in the above prophecies, one should look at the possibility of their happening by chance. Could this have been done by man, or was there divine intervention? Here is a basic list of some of the criteria:

1. You would have had to select the correct virgin from all the maidens who were from the tribe of Judah, and specifically from the house of David.

2. You would have had to know in advance the gender of the Child she would conceive.

3. You would have had previous knowledge of the name of the Child.

4. Immanuel means that God would come to us in the form of the Messiah.

As you can see, the odds of these events happening by chance are too astronomical to be done by man. This could only be fulfilled by Someone outside of space and time.

It is very interesting that God has encoded the name of the Messiah and the virgin within the area of Isaiah 7:13-14. But, I will say more on this in a later chapter.

PATRIARCHS AND MATRIARCHS

In all of this, God would have to bring forth a holy nation that did not exist during the time from Adam to Jacob. The Lord put in motion the genealogy that would produce this nation. It started with Adam all the way through Noah, then on through Abraham. Abraham had two sons, Ishmael and Isaac. Isaac, the son of promise, was selected by God to be the father of Jacob, who later had his name changed to Israel. Israel would become a great nation that God would use to fulfill His prophecies concerning the Messiah.

Most of the following information is cryptically encoded in the first two chapters of Genesis. This is truly the foreknowledge of our all-knowing God in action.

Genesis 1:22. *God blessed them, saying, be fruitful and multiply.* From this Scripture we have a prophetic picture of God's ultimate purpose in the patriarch Abraham.

Genesis 1:22. Starting with the first letter in the third word, counting forward every 50th letter spells *Abraham; Avraham;* אברהם. Abraham was chosen by God to be the father of many nations. Not only is Abraham encoded at 50-ELS, but Sarah; שרה, his wife, as well.

An analysis was done on this code, and the percentages of

this happening by chance in the first chapter of Genesis are less than .004 to 1,000,000 (one million).

The Scripture reference that Abraham would be a father of many nations is found in Genesis 17.

Genesis 17:1-5, 15. (1) *And when Abram was ninety years old and nine, the LORD appeared to Abram, and said unto him, I am the Almighty God; walk before me, and be thou perfect. (2) And I will make my covenant between me and thee, and will multiply thee exceedingly. (3) And Abram fell on his face: and God talked with him, saying, (4) As for me, behold, my covenant is with thee, and thou shalt be a father of many nations. (5) Neither shall thy name any more be called Abram, but thy name shall be [אברהם] Abraham; for a father of many nations have I made thee. (15) And God said unto Abraham, As for Sarai thy wife, thou shalt not call her name Sarai, but Sarah [שרה] shall her name be.*

It never ceases to amaze me that God has given us advanced information by the surface reading as well as the hidden treasures within His Word, revealing His absolute foreknowledge of all things. The Bible codes should be considered from a heavenly perspective, not from a secular position. Though there are many codes that deal with the secular, nevertheless, they should be viewed from the prophetic standpoint. This is especially true, since the individuals and events were all encoded long before they came to pass on the earthly scene.

The names of all the patriarchs and matriarchs are encoded within the first two chapters of Genesis. The patriarchs are

Abraham, Isaac, and *Jacob;* the matriarchs are *Sarah, Rebecca, Leah,* and *Rachel.* What is so mind-boggling is that even all the tribes of Israel, the sons of Jacob, are meticulously placed throughout these same chapters of Genesis. Not only the wives of the patriarchs are encoded, but also their concubines, *Hagar, Zilpah,* and *Bilhah.*

The Lord gave Abraham and Sarah many promises that are still in the process of being fulfilled. He also gave Hagar promises, many of which are yet to come to pass. After Hagar and her son *Ishmael;* ישמעאל, which means *God heard,* were driven away from Abraham, they became lost while wandering in the wilderness. Both mother and son were on the verge of dying from thirst and exposure. Hagar cried out to the Lord, and God heard her and Ishmael's pleas for help. The Lord sent His angel to her and gave her promises from God; in addition, He showed her the location of a well.

Genesis 21:17. *And God heard [וישמע אלהים] the voice of the lad; and the angel of God called to Hagar out of heaven, and said unto her, What aileth thee, Hagar? fear not; for God hath heard the voice of the lad where he is.*

Notice the name of Ishmael; ישמעאל is in the phrase, *and God heard;* וישמע אלהים. The Lord had compassion on Hagar and her son and was completely aware of their dreadful situation.

Years later, Hagar's son Ishmael became the father of twelve sons and a daughter, and most of their names are encoded within the first chapter of Genesis. We must remember that they also were of the natural seed of Abraham. The same Messiah who will bless Israel also will bless the offsprings of Hagar.

THE TORAH

Throughout her existence, Israel had suffered many hardships, but God had always provided a solution for every circumstance, even when Israel was in rebellion against the commandments of God. The Lord set guidelines and restrictions for His beloved nation. However, it was not just for His own benefit, but also for the benefit of Israel.

The first five books of Moses are Genesis, Exodus, Leviticus, Numbers, and Deuteronomy. All the names of these books are encoded at various intervals throughout the first chapter of Genesis. As a matter of fact, all but three of the books of the Old Testament are encoded there. Fifty days after Moses led the whole house of Israel out of Egypt from bondage, God called him up to the top of Mount Sinai, where he was instructed by the Lord to write the Torah, commonly called the five books of Moses.

Starting in the first word of the Torah, we have an embedded description of certain things referring to that memorial day when Moses ascended the mountain.

Genesis 1:1. Starting with the sixth letter in the first word, counting forward every 50th letter spells *the Law; Torah*; תורה. If you continue counting every 50th letter, you will find the writer Moses; משה; and the tribe Levi; לוי, from which he came. Also, the

Hebrew word for *record (make a record)*; *rashem*; רשם is encoded next to his name—all at 50-ELS.

One of the codes in this 50-letter matrix that really gets my attention contains the phrase, *Behold, the love of the Father; ha aohav aba*; הא אהב אבא. No matter who we are, or whatever our circumstances, we can always know that God really does love us.

When Moses ascended Mount Sinai, he requested of God that he may see His goodness. God granted Moses' request by demonstrating His love and kindness to him. The Lord hid him in the cleft of the rock; then He passed by Moses. When Moses looked up, he saw the afterglow of His consummate love and holiness. That was more than sufficient for Moses. Later, it is recorded that Moses was the meekest man on earth. The presence of almighty God humbles anyone, unless you have a rebellious heart.

Since Abraham was the father of many nations, and Jacob was the father of Israel, you might be wondering whether God encoded the name of the nation from where the Messiah would come. Well, He has done just that. In Genesis 1:30, starting with the second letter in the ninth word, counting forward every 50th letter spells *greatness to Israel; el rav Yisrael*; אל רב ישראל. This is a prophetic code that deals with the future of the offsprings of Jacob and the nation of Israel. I hasten to inform the reader that God also has many awesome blessings for the Arabs and all the other nations of this world.

A computer expert did a mathematical analysis on this particular encoded phrase as found within the limits of the first two chapters of Genesis. To our amazement, approximate odds came out to be less than 0.00000 to 1,000,000 (one million). *Standard deviation:* 2019.10. This gives us the odds of less than 1 to 1,000,000,000,000 (one trillion). Better said, it is literally impossible for the above codes to have taken place by chance.

Then the expert challenged the whole Torah for a duplicate appearance of the same, but to no avail. In Genesis 1 and 2 is the only place this combination is cryptically encoded at 50-letter intervals. What does all this prove? Simply this: that God is the author of His own Word, and that it would have been impossible for man to have composed such an arrayed structure of letters, words, and books that are interlocked with corresponding letters, words, and phrases.

The Holy Bible has an uniquely mathematical arrangement that is unequaled in any of the other writings in the whole world. This wonderful Book has a depth of truth and cryptic coding that has no limit. I can tell you, unhesitatingly, that if you read just the plain structure or search for the hidden manna, it cannot be compared with the very best of books that have been written since time began. Let me give you some additional examples.

The *Torah* is encoded at 50-letter intervals at the beginning of Genesis, Exodus, Numbers, and at 49-letter intervals in Deuteronomy. *Torah* appears with reverse spelling in Numbers and Deuteronomy. All four of these point to the central book, Leviticus. However, when you go to the precise center of the Torah (Leviticus 8:29), another phenomenon takes place.

In the exact center—the very core—of the Torah, which is the 152,403rd letter, within the phrase where this central letter is located, *He is;* הוא (the midsection of the 304,805 letters), I found the name *Jehovah;* יהוה encoded at 50-letter intervals. *He is the heart of His Word and the Wheel-within-the-wheel.*

ISRAEL AND THE PERSECUTION OF THE JEWS

After Israel became a holy nation and they were in their own land, many of the nations persecuted them beyond human endurance. The record shows that when Israel was rebellious toward God they were harassed by other nations. Six powerful empires rose up during the beginnings of this tiny nation. Egypt was the first nation to persecute Israel and, therefore, held them in bondage for a period of 200 years or more, though they had been in Egypt for 430 years.

After Egypt, it was the Assyrians who dispersed the tribes, torturing those they held in captivity. Then came the Babylonians, who took them away to Babylon and held them captive for seventy years. After the Babylonian Empire was defeated by Medo-Persia, they in turn held them at the point of the sword. The Grecian Empire, under Alexander the Great, conquered ten nations in the Middle East, including the Medo-Persian Empire. After the death of Alexander, his four generals took power over the Grecian Empire. General Seleucus was given Israel, Syria, and Babylonia. The Roman Empire conquered all the known world of that day, including Israel. These are the six empires that conquered and persecuted the tiny nation of Israel for over

2,000 years. Although Israel did enjoy peace from time to time, especially under King David and Solomon, it was short-lived.

All six of these nations are encoded in Genesis 1, within the diameter of another code that spells *Israel.*

Genesis 1:1. Starting with the third letter in the third word, counting forward every 232nd letter spells *Israel to inherit (possess); Yisrael ve' yaresh;* ישׂראל וירשׁ.

In spite of the many hostilities from surrounding countries as well as from within that Israel has suffered throughout the centuries, even to this modern day, Holy Scripture is clear that *she will survive* as a nation and inherit the blessings that God promised Abraham, Isaac, and Jacob. These promises can only be fulfilled by God's Messiah, *the Son of David.*

Joshua; Yehoshua; יהושׁע was a type of Messiah who brought the sons of Israel to the promised land. His name means *salvation of the Lord.* There were many battles along the way, but the Israelites *prevailed in the name of the Lord.* When Joshua took them to the seemingly impregnable walls of the pagan city of Jericho, little did those who dwelt there know that their famous walls would come tumbling down by the blowing of the shophars [trumpets] and the shouts of all the people of Israel. It wasn't the shout that brought them down, but *the power of God* behind the shout. Joshua believed God; therefore, he brought Israel all the way to the land that God had given to Abraham, *winning every battle and praising the Lord all the way.*

After they crossed over the flooded Jordan River, an event

which was against all odds of their survival, they kept the *Passover*. This was on the 14th day of the month of Aviv, which was commanded by the Lord. By keeping the commandment of the Passover, they set in motion a standard that was to be observed in their own land throughout the history of Israel. Had they not crossed over Jordan and kept the *Passover*, there would have been no Israel nor a Messiah for their future deliverance. But they *believed God* and went forward.

Joshua 5:10. *And the children of Israel encamped in Gilgal, and kept the passover on the fourteenth day of the month at even in the plains of Jericho.* This verse provides another revealing insight that demonstrates the power of His precious Word.

The mathematical value of the name *Israel; Yisrael;* ישראל is 541. The Hebrew spelling of the name Israel means *uprightness in God.* All things in the Bible are significant. Never underestimate the cogency of each letter and His Word. In Joshua 5:10, starting with the first letter in the tenth word, counting forward every 541st letter spells *Israel; Yisrael;* ישראל.

After they crossed over Jordan and approached the walls of Jericho, God told Joshua to command seven priests to blow seven shophars while walking around the walls every day for seven days. The army of Israel marched before them and the Ark of the Covenant, and the rest of the people followed them, walking behind the Ark. The order was the army, the priests, the Ark, and then the people.

By doing this God's way, the Ark of the Lord was in the

midst of all the people of Israel. They were commanded to be silent, except for the blowing of the trumpets during the seventh trip around the walls on the seventh day. Perhaps the first six trips around the walls allude to the six thousand years before the Messiah sets up the seventh dispensation, which will last for 1,000 years. Then all of the enemies of God and His people will be destroyed and come tumbling down.

Joshua 6:16, 20. (16) *And it came to pass at the seventh time, when the priests blew with the trumpets, Joshua said unto the people, Shout; for the LORD hath given you the city. (20) So the people shouted when the priests blew with the trumpets: and it came to pass, when the people heard the sound of the trumpet, and the people shouted with a great shout, that the wall fell down flat, so that the people went up into the city, every man straight before him, and they took the city.*

Regarding the walls of Jericho, Grant Jeffrey gives the following archeological fact:

During excavations of Jericho between 1930 and 1936, Professor John Garstang found one of the most incredible confirmations of the biblical record about the conquest of the Promised Land. The results were so amazing that he took the precaution of preparing a written declaration of the archeological discovery, signed by himself and two other members of his team. "As to the main fact, then, there remains no doubt: the walls fell outwards so completely that the attackers would be able to clamber up and over their ruins into the city." This fact is important because the evidence from all other archeological digs around ancient cities in the Middle East reveal that walls of cities always fall inwards as invading armies push their way into a city. However, in the account in Joshua 6:20, we read, "the wall fell down flat, so that the people went up into the city every man straight ahead, and they took the city." Only the supernatural power of God could have caused the walls to fall outward as described in Joshua's account of the conquest of Jericho (John Garstang, Joshua Judges, [London: Constable, 1931]).[3]

After Israel settled in their own land, which was given to them by God, they went the way of unbelievers. So, the Lord used other nations to get their attention. King David, the second king of Israel, reunited all the tribes into one nation and ruled for a total of forty years. Finally, Solomon, the son of David, was given the privilege of building the first Temple, the house where God would dwell. Ironically, the names of *Moses* and *Solomon* along with *Tabernacle* and *Temple* are encoded in the second chapter of Genesis. It also contains *the Ark* and *God; Elohim.* The names of the pillars and all of the articles that were used in the Tabernacle and Temple services also are located in chapter one.

However, in Genesis 2:4, starting with the fourth letter in

---

[3]Grant Jeffrey, *The Signature of God* (Toronto: Frontier Research Publishing, 1994), pp. 74-75. Used by permission.

the eighth word, counting forward every 18th letter spells *Temple...Tabernacle* (together); היכלהאה. Reading this from right to left spells *Temple; haikal;* היכל. But when this same combination is read from left to right, it spells *the Tabernacle; ha'ohail;* האהל. Now, as you read from left to right *all* of the above code, it says, *the Tabernacle (dwelling place) for the Lord.* This is quite interesting by itself, but *Moses;* משה also shows up at the 18-ELS count and *Solomon;* שלמה at 15-ELS count. These insights are profound and prophetic in nature. Who, but God, could have instructed Moses to write the letters comprising the Torah?

The names of the two nations that were instrumental in destroying Jerusalem, and the two Temples are also encoded in the immediate area. Rome; *Romai;* רומאי at 19-ELS count and *Babylon; Babel;* בבל at 15-ELS count.

Solomon's Temple was destroyed by the Babylonians in 586 B.C.; the second Temple, commonly called Herod's Temple, was destroyed by the Romans in 70 A.D. From the time of the destruction of the second Temple to this present day, Israel has been persecuted and driven beyond endurance. The worst of these offenders were the Nazis during World War II. Hitler and his cohorts did their very best to exterminate the Jews as well as anyone who was partial to them.

Some years ago, certain Israeli scientists did a comprehensive computer analysis in the Hebrew Masoretic Text for information concerning the World War II holocaust, the death camps, and the participants. It is quite amazing what they found.

Deuteronomy 10:17. Starting with the first letter in the ninth word, counting forward every 22nd letter spells *Hitler; Heetlair* היטלר, which is the name of the leader of the Nazi party. However, one must remember that there were 22 men tried at the Nuremburg trials, but only ten were hanged.

Deuteronomy 10:20. Starting with the first letter in the seventh word, counting in reverse every 13th letter spells *Auschwitz;* אושויץ. I continued the search, and the whole statement reads as follows, *in the bitter sea of Auschwitz;* בים מרה אושויץ.

Auschwitz is located in Poland and was one of the most terrible death camps ever to exist in the history of mankind. Many Jewish people received the Lord while imprisoned within these concentration camps. Ironically, we can find the name of the Messiah encoded in this section of Scripture.

My good Jewish friend was living in Poland at the time of the invasion on September 1939. Later, he was taken to one of the death camps in Poland. He was moved to other camps, a total of twenty-two in all. Then he was sent to the Treblinka work camp for the duration of the war. It was here, during the many trying days of persecution, that he called out to the Lord God of Israel.

After many of his friends died while in the prison, he resigned himself to the situation and turned his life over to the Lord. Miraculously, he survived and is now living in the United States. He has shared with me many of his experiences while he was incarcerated by the Nazis. Talking to him today, you would never know that he had suffered so much by so many. He has a forgiving attitude toward everyone, even the Nazis.

We are approaching a time in history when the persecution will take place again, but in an unprecedented and unusual way. This time, it will engulf the entire globe, and all who will not bend their knee to the last days' regime will be singled out and persecuted beyond measure. It will be a time of anti-Jewish and anti-Christian hatred and violence, eventually culminating in the setting up of the Messianic kingdom on earth.

We have a God who cares for and loves *all of us*. He will not leave us nor forsake us, no matter what the circumstances may be.

Three

THE COMPUTER AGE

Knowledge in the information age of the twenty-first century is growing exponentially, and studies reveal that it is doubling every four months. The computer microchip, which is an integrated circuit designed to process information with enormous speed and accuracy, enhances man's ability to advance rapidly in the various fields of technology and education.

Just how very small this invention is was dramatically illustrated in the October 1982 issue of *National Geographic*. On page 131, there is a photograph (17x magnification) of a large ant, gripping with its jaws a tiny computer microprocessor—the "chip." On the front cover of this same issue is a photograph of a chip resting in the huge palm of a man's hand. How far advanced have they gone with this technology to date? It is difficult to say because there are many fields of experimentation progressing at a rapid pace, all at the same time. Recently published reports quoting technology sources reveal plans for designs of even smaller and more powerful microchips, some of which would be composed of a soft, gelatin-like material.

Was all this prophesied in the Bible? I believe so. When we go to the book of Daniel, we find many end-time scenarios that deal with our modern day's rapidly increasing knowledge and travel.

Daniel 12:1-4, 9. (1) *And at that time shall Michael stand up, the great prince which standeth for the children of thy people: and there shall be a time of trouble, such as never was since there was a nation even to that same time: and at that time thy people shall be delivered, every one that shall be found written in the book. (2) And many of them that sleep in the dust of the earth shall awake, some to everlasting life, and some to shame and everlasting contempt. (3) And they that be wise shall shine as the brightness of the firmament; and they that turn many to righteousness as the stars for ever and ever. (4) But thou, O Daniel, shut up the words, and seal the book, even to the time of the end: many shall run to and fro, and knowledge shall be increased. (9) And he said, Go thy way, Daniel: for the words are closed up and sealed till the time of the end.*

There are seven major thoughts from these Scriptures I want to bring to light.

1. Michael, the great prince for Israel, shall stand up.

2. It will be the time of the end.

3. Knowledge and travel shall increase.

4. It will be a time of trouble as never before since there was a nation.

5. He that wins souls is wise, and the righteous shall shine as the stars forever and ever.

6. The sealed words of this prophecy will be opened at the end of time.

7. God's people shall be delivered in this time frame. Also, the righteous dead shall be resurrected.

Daniel 12:6. Starting with the fifth letter in the fourth word, counting in reverse every 30th letter spells *computer on line; machaiv le'kav;* מחשב לקו. This biblical Hebrew word means *an invention; (to) calculate,* but in the modern Hebrew it means *computer.* The phrase, *computer on line,* is a fact of this age. For this to show up in the Scripture referring to the end-time is quite significant. The adjacent letters at the same ELS spell *the knowledge of science;* המדע. Also, COBOL, one of the languages the computer uses, is encoded in this same area.

The encoded word for *computer* crosses over another word that is related to the computer, *the image; ha'tzelam;* הצלם. The computer produces an image on a screen, and that same image can be printed on paper. Also, it can be transmitted anywhere in the world where there is an interchangeable system. In this same matrix, the word *robot; golem;* גולם is encoded. All of the robotic machinery in the world is controlled by some type of computer. However, this is a prophetic picture that has been drawn from the pages of prophecy to describe a scenario of the end-time when an evil one will make an image of himself and cause everyone in the world to bow down and worship it.

The prophet Daniel was told by the angel that many shall run to and fro at the time of the end. Never before in the history of the world has man traveled at such unparalleled speed. It has become a way of life—flying or driving from one place to another. Distance poses no barrier for this generation. Not only have we advanced in the field of travel but in communication as well. If I want to send electronic mail (Email) to all of my subscribers at the same time, it is no task at all. Just push the key and they all receive the information at lightning speed.

Within these Scriptures the *Messiah* is encoded, including His name, which I will discuss at great length in the next chapter. In Daniel 12:7, starting with the sixth letter in the 20th word, counting forward every 20th letter spells *Messiah; Mashiach;* משיח. Since it will be the time of great deliverance in the end, it only seems logical that His name would be encoded here.

Daniel is not the only place in the Scriptures where these encoded phenomena take place. In many of the prophecies we find these same occurrences and additional information on the same subject.

AS IT WERE IN THE DAYS OF NOAH

When Daniel prophesied of the time of the end, he did not have available to him the New Testament prophecies concerning this same subject. However, much of what he wrote is spoken of again in the book of Matthew and other sections of the New Testament.

Matthew 24:21-24, 37. (21) *For then shall be great tribulation, such as was not since the beginning of the world to this time, no, nor ever shall be. (22) And except those days should be short-*

ened, there should no flesh be saved: but for the elect's sake those days shall be shortened. (23) Then if any man shall say unto you, Lo, here is Christ [Messiah], or there; believe it not. (24) For there shall arise false Christs, and false prophets, and shall show great signs and wonders; insomuch that, if it were possible, they shall deceive the very elect. (37) But as the days of Noah were, so shall also the coming of the Son of man [Messiah] be.

Notice that the Word says *as the days of Noah were.* To receive a better understanding of this prophecy we need to look in Genesis chapter six and compare the pre-flood period with today's conditions. We can see a parallel of events that are unprecedented in the annals of history.

Genesis 6:5. *And God saw that the wickedness of man was great in the earth, and that every imagination of the thoughts of his heart was only evil continually.*

God was fully aware of their evil deeds in Noah's day. But when you compare his era with today, we see horrible corresponding events.

Genesis 6:6-9. (6) *And it repented the LORD that he had made man on the earth, and it grieved him at his heart. (7) And the LORD said, I will destroy man whom I have created from the face of the earth; both man, and beast, and the creeping thing, and the fowls of the air; for it repenteth me that I have made them. (8) But Noah found grace in the eyes of the LORD. (9) These are the generations of Noah: Noah was a just man and perfect in his generations, and Noah walked with God.*

6 וינחם יהוה כי־עשה את־האדם בארץ ויתעצב אל־לבו:

7 ויאמר יהוה אמחה את־האדם אשר־בראתי מעל פני

האדמה מאדם עד־בהמה עד־רמש ועד־עוף השמים כי

נחמתי כי עשיתם: 8 ונח מצא חן בעיני יהוה:

9 אלה תולדת נח נח איש צדיק תמים היה בדרתיו

את־האלהים התהלך־נח:

To reflect on some of the insights encoded in this portion of Scripture, I want to show you the hidden codes that lie beneath the surface reading.

Genesis 6:9. Starting with the sixth letter in the 11th word, counting in reverse every 30th letter spells *strange (peculiar) computer; machshaiv tah'mu'ah;* מחשב תמוה. The Hebrew word, *tah'-mu'ah*, can also mean *unusual* or *out of the ordinary*. The adjacent letters at the same ELS spell *invent (devise) knowledge; bada dai'ah;* בדא דע. This is the same count that is encoded in Daniel 12, reflecting Daniel's words *that knowledge shall increase in the last days.*

This is one of the capabilities of the modern-day computer, especially the supercomputer. The computer is being used for the glory of God, but the enemy of the righteousness of God has taken this unique instrument to use it for the vilest of lusts and murderous evil.

The portion of this Scripture that stands out in my mind is the fact that Noah walked with God. There are many people today who are like Noah; they love and walk with God and find grace in His eyes. Remember, it says that as it were in the days of

Noah, so shall it be in the coming of the Messiah. It is our God-given duty to proclaim the *Good News* to every person everywhere with every available means at our disposal.

NIMROD AND THE ANCIENT TOWER OF BABEL

Now, consider the following set of facts very carefully. The European Economic Community (European Union is its official name) is a group of countries that have come under the same *military, political, and monetary head.* Since the days of the Roman Empire, many conquerors have unsuccessfully tried to unify Europe under one head. In 800 A.D., Charlemagne could not succeed. Napoleon met his Waterloo over 1,000 years later. Mussolini and Hitler made an attempt, but they were defeated by the Allies during World War II.

What all these great empires lacked in their goals for a unified Europe was the *fulfillment* of biblical prophecies that speak of the *revised* Roman Empire coming into power in the last days before the end of this age. Significantly, one of the two *emblems* the European Union uses is the Tower of Babel. In order to understand the significance of that emblem, we must look at the similarities of the two—the other, designated by a certain, three-digit number.

In Genesis 10:8, the Scripture gives us the name of the founder of the city of Babel and the religion of Babylon. Nimrod was the son of Cush and grandson of Ham. Some scholars believe this evil man had a genius intellect that surpassed our modern-day brain capacity. In Genesis 11:6, the Lord describes

Babylon's spiritual decay and open blasphemy against Him, perpetrated by Nimrod and his occultic religion. These same occultic tentacles have survived to this day and are running rampant in our modern societies across the world.

Genesis 10:8-10. (8) *And Cush begat Nimrod: he began to be a mighty one in the earth. (9) He was a mighty hunter before the LORD: wherefore it is said, Even as Nimrod the mighty hunter before the LORD. (10) And the beginning of his kingdom was Babel, and Erech, and Accad, and Calneh, in the land of Shinar.*

8 וכוש ילד את־נמרד הוא החל להיות גבר בארץ:

9 הוא־היה גבר־ציד לפני יהוה על־כן יאמר כנמרד

גבור ציד לפני יהוה: 10 נתהי ראשית ממלכתו

בבל וארך ואכד וכלנה בארץ שנער:

Nimrod was the founder of four cities that have distinct meanings. 1. Babel; *confusion.* 2. Erech; *length.* 3. Accad; *strengthen; fortress.* 4. Calneh; *murmuring.* These cities he established in the land of Shinar, which is 600 miles east of Jerusalem and on the plains of Babylon. One of the meanings of Shinar is *the changing of a city.*

Many years later, Babylon became a great nation that ultimately ruled the world of that day. The religion of Babylon was an offshoot of Nimrod's occultic beliefs, which permeated all walks of life—civil and religious. It was an evil, perverted light. Frequently, the devil (Satan) masquerades as an angel of light to deceive and capture the souls of men.

In these final days, the religion of Babylon is now beginning to show its horns of deception. It is rapidly becoming that last and most evil form of religion on the face of the earth. Emanating from its dark and secret core, it extends its influences throughout the secular arts and entertainment community as well as in many political and certain religious organizations. Consequently, its tenets of faith, by way of its brainwashed "ministers" of "spiritual humanism," have been blaspheming man and God.

There are dynamic encoded insights within these areas of Scripture, which were recorded in the Masoretic Hebrew many thousands of years ago.

Genesis 10:8. Starting with the third letter in the fifth word, counting in reverse every 13th letter spells *evil (perverse) light; avon ohr;* אור עון. Also, adjacent to this phrase at 13-ELS is another one that depicts the result of *evil light.* In Genesis 10:9, starting with the first letter in the fifth word, counting every 13th letter in reverse spells *oppressions; distresses; afflictions; lah'chatzim;* לחחים.

During the time of the reign of the *false messiah (antichrist),* he will impose a mark (the other emblem) on all who follow him in his diabolical scheme to take over Israel and the world. One of the identities of the false messiah will be the number, 666. His kingdom will be organized similar to the previous empires that persecuted Israel.

This means that every person under the domain of the *false messiah* will be required to receive this mark. For many years, this was impossible, but since the advent of the *supercomputer,* which has been called *the modern tower of Babel* because it has been programmed to "speak" many technical languages, a whole new world of technological marvels, along with the potential for abuse, is emerging.

Genesis 11:1-9. (1) *And the whole earth was of one language, and of one speech.* (2) *And it came to pass, as they journeyed from the east, that they found a plain in the land of Shinar; and they dwelt there.* (3) *And they said one to another, Go to, let us make brick, and burn them thoroughly. And they had brick for stone, and slime had they for mortar.* (4) *And they said, Go to, let us build us a city and a tower, whose top may reach unto heaven; and let us make us a name, lest we be scattered abroad upon the face of the whole earth.* (5) *And the LORD came down to see the city and the tower, which the children of men builded.* (6) *And the LORD said, Behold, the people is one, and they have all one language; and this they begin to do: and now nothing will be restrained from them, which they have imagined to do.* (7) *Go to, let us go down, and there confound their language, that they may not understand one another's speech.* (8) *So the LORD scattered them abroad from thence upon the face of all the earth: and they left off to build the city.* (9) *Therefore is the name of it called Babel; because the LORD did there confound the language of all the earth: and from thence did the LORD scatter them abroad upon the face of all the earth.*

1 ויהי כל־הארץ שפה אחת ודברים אחדים:

2 ויהי בנסעם מקדם וימצאו בקעה בארץ שנער וישבו שם:

3 ויאמרו איש אל־רעהו הבה נלבנה לבנים ונשרפה לשרפה

ותהי להם הלבנה לאבן והחמר היה להם לחמר:

4 ויאמרו הבה נבנה־לנו עיר ומגדל וראשו בשמים.

ונעשה־לנו שם פן־נפוץ על־פני כל־הארץ:

5 וירד יהוה לראת את־־העיר ואת־המגדל אשר בנו בני האדם:

6 ויאמר יהוה הן עם אחד ושפה אחת לכלם וזה החלם

לעשות ועתה לא־יבצר מהם כל אמר יזמו לעשות:

7 הבה נרדה ונבלה שם שפתם אשר לא ישמעו איש שפת רעהו:

8 ויפץ יהוה אתם משם על־פני כל־הארץ ויחדלו לבנת העיר:

9 על־כן קרא שמה בבל כי־שם בלל יהוה שפת כל־הארץ

ומשם היצם יהוה על־פני כל־הארץ:

This gives us a picture of the mindset of those ancient people. The evil imagination of mankind was getting out of control as they started to build a tower, the top of which was to reach into the heavens. So deceived by their arrogance and greed, they apparently believed they could challenge their Creator so as not to cause another worldwide flood, such as occurred in Noah's day. If God did send another flood in the proportions of Noah's day, they believed they could have a refuge of their own building. Read Genesis chapters 6 through 8.

Genesis 11:2. Starting with the fourth letter in the fifth word, counting in reverse every 13th letter spells *the computer*; *ha'machshaiv*; המחשב.

Encoded within this area of Scripture in Genesis chapter 11 are many names of cities or countries that will play a part in the end-time scenario, plus other information revealing some things that will take place then. The names of these nations are found at various places throughout the Bible, and especially when the Scripture is referring to the last days, during which time the *false messiah* comes on the scene to fulfill his hellish schemes.

1. Babel; בבל -13.

2. Euphrates; פרת + 13.

3. The river of Ba'al; בל הנהר + 10.

4. The lion of the end to prophesy; היא ארי בקץ הנבא + 6. This insight represents Babylon, which has a mouth like a lion and speaks many blasphemies against God in the last days.

5. Devastation; שאוה + 7.

6. Libyans; לבי + 13.

7. Cush (Ethiopia); כוש -13.

8. Greece; יון + 15.

9. Egypt; מצרים -17.

10. Medes; מדי + 2.

11. Assyria; אשור -47.

12. Syria; אמר -23. Adjacent letters spell *fire of deceit*; מרמה האש.

13. Evil serpent; נחש ער -15.

14. Gomorrah; עמרה -13.

15. Persia (Iran); פרס -161.

16. Proud (insolent) Roman; רומי זוד -135.

Though the supercomputer was meant for good, it will be used as part of Satan's Machiavellian scheme to enslave the whole world. Although many computers on a global scale *may* fail in the near future because of the wide variety of viruses that are on the loose, this powerful supercomputer, ultimately, will be virus free and will be used by the *anti-Messiah system,* enabling its emissaries to number and control all aspects of life during the time of trouble (the great tribulation) that was predicted by the Holy Bible.

Some of the combinations that I found encoded in this same area of Scripture are insights pertaining to the coming of Messiah when He sets up the Messianic kingdom. For instance, in Genesis 11:13-15, we find the genealogy of the forefathers of King David, who was a type of Messiah.

Genesis 11:13-15. (13) *And Arphaxad lived after he begat [fathered] Salah four hundred and three years, and begat sons and daughters.* (14) *And Salah lived thirty years, and begat Eber.* (15) *And Salah lived after he begat Eber four hundred and three years, and begat sons and daughters.*

Genesis 11:10. Starting with the fifth letter in the tenth word, counting forward every 14th letter spells *David;* דוד. This Scripture gives us some detail about the royal bloodline of the Messiah, of which David's was a part.

Genesis 11:13. Starting with the second letter in the first word, counting forward every tenth letter spells *unity of Messiah; yachad Mashiach;* יחד משׁיח. The name of the Messiah is also encoded adjacent to David and Messiah, which I will discuss in great detail later in the book.

Many agnostics do not believe there ever was a Tower of Babel constructed by a man called Nimrod. Some people refuse to accept biblical truth because they would have to change their way of life and perhaps be rejected by their peers. In these last days, many archeologists' diggings have uncovered concrete evidence that such a place did exist. In fact, there are other fascinating historical sites—too numerous to mention—that reveal the biblical accounts of ancient history.

For anyone who wonders about the historical validity, Grant Jeffrey provides us with research regarding King Nebuchadnezzar's inscription about the Tower of Babel.

From the time of Adam and Eve, "The whole earth had one language and one speech" (Genesis 11:1), before the dispersion of the population following God's supernatural act causing the confusion of their languages at the Tower of Babel. God purposely confounded the language of all the people on the earth (Genesis 11:9) so they could not understand the speech of their neighbors to force them to disperse throughout the earth. The people had gathered together in sinful pride against God in their attempt to build a tower that would reach to the heavens. Moses recorded God's subsequent judgment and destruction of the Tower of Babel and the city of Babylon. The remains of the Tower of Babel are vitrified (melted to form a kind of rough glass) which indicates that was erected at the dawn of time by men in their sinful pride to reach up to the heavens in defiance of God. Scientists who study the origin of languages, known as philologists, have concluded that it is probable that the thousands of dialects and languages throughout the planet can be traced back to an original language in man's ancient past. Professor Alfredo Trombetti claims that he can prove the common origin of all languages. Max Mueller, one of the greatest oriental language scholars, declared that all human languages can be traced back to one single original language. Professor Otto Jespersen stated that the first language was given to man by God.

The French government sent Professor Oppert to report on the cuneiform inscriptions discovered in the ruins of Babylon. Oppert translated a long inscription by King Nebuchadnezzar in which the king referred to the tower in the Chaldean language as Barzippa, which means Tongue-tower. The Greeks used the word Borsippa, with the same meaning of tongue-tower, to describe the ruins of the Tower of Babel. This inscription of Nebuchadnezzar clearly identified the original tower of Borsippa with the Tower of Babel described by Moses in Genesis. King Nebuchadnezzar decided to rebuild the base of the ancient Tower of Babel, built over sixteen centuries earlier by Nimrod, the first King of Babylon. He also called it the Temple of the Spheres. During the millennium since God destroyed it, the tower was reduced from its original height and magnificence until only the huge base of the tower (four hundred and sixty feet by six hundred and ninety feet) standing some two hundred and seventy-five feet high remained within the outskirts of the city of Babylon. Today the ruins have been reduced to about one hundred and fifty feet above the plain with a circumference of 2,300 feet.

Nebuchadnezzar rebuilt the city of Babylon in great magnificence with gold and silver, and then decided to rebuild the lowest platform of the Tower of Babel in honor of the Chaldean gods. King Nebuchadnezzar resurfaced the base of the Tower of Babel with gold, silver, cedar, and fir, at great cost on top of a hard seal of Nebuchadnezzar. [A photograph of one of these Babylonian bricks created by Nebuchadnezzar is included in the photo section.] In this inscription found on the base of the ruins of the Tower of Babel, King Nebuchadnezzar speaks in his own words from thousands of years ago confirming one of the most interesting events of the ancient past.

KING NEBUCHADNEZZAR'S INSCRIPTION FOUND ON THE TOWER OF BABEL

The tower, the eternal house, which I founded and built. I have completed its magnificence with silver, gold, and other metals, stone, enameled bricks, fir and pine.

The first which is the house of the earth's base, the most ancient monument of Babylon; I built and finished it.

I have highly exalted its head with bricks covered with copper.

We say for the other, that is, this edifice, the house of the seven lights of the earth, the most ancient monument of Borsippa.

A former king built it, (they reckon 42 ages) but he did not complete its head.

Since a remote time, people had abandoned it, without order expressing their words.

Since that time the earthquake and the thunder had dispersed the sun-dried clay.

The bricks of the casing had been split, and the earth of the interior had been scattered in heaps. Merodach, the great god, excited my mind to repair this building.

I did not change the site nor did I take away the foundation.

In a fortunate month, in an auspicious day,

I undertook to build porticoes around the crude brick masses, and the casing of burnt bricks.

I adapted the circuits, I put the inscription of my name in the Kitir of the portico.

I set my hand to finish it. And to exalt its head.

As it had been in ancient days, so I exalted its summit.

This inscription was translated by Professor Oppert. In addition, Mr. William Loftus translated this fascinating inscription in his book, *Travels and Researches in Chaldea and Sinai*. This incredible inscription confirms the biblical accuracy of one of the most fascinating stories in the Book of Genesis. The pagan king Nebuchadnezzar confirms in his own words the incredible details that "a former king built it, but he did not complete its head," confirming the truthfulness of the Genesis account that God stopped the original builders from completing the top of the Tower of Babel. Most significantly, King Nebuchadnezzar's inscription declares that the reason the original king could not complete the tower was because, "Since a remote time, people had abandoned it, without order expressing their words." In other words, they lost the ability to control their language and communication![4]

---

[4]Grant Jeffrey, *The Signature of God* (Toronto: Frontier Research Publishing, 1994), pp. 38-41.

JEREMIAH, THE WEEPING PROPHET

The prophet Jeremiah was contemporary with the prophet Daniel, who also prophesied concerning Israel and their downfall and their salvation. One of the major prophecies of Jeremiah was that Babylon would conquer Israel, who would go into captivity for seventy years. This prophecy came to pass exactly as the Lord had instructed Jeremiah. Some of the predictions that Jeremiah made were the terrible events that would take place in the last days.

Jeremiah was called the *weeping prophet*, because he wept for Israel and the gloom and destruction that was coming upon her. Jeremiah refers to Babylon many times throughout his book. One of the most dynamic predictions is found in Jeremiah chapter 25. In this prophecy, Jeremiah refers to the existing kingdoms of *his* day, then he refers to *all* the kingdoms in the whole world. This prophecy leaps forward to the end of time when the nations will be drunk with the spiritual fornication of Mystery Babylon.

Jeremiah 25:13-17. (13) *And I will bring upon that land all my words which I have pronounced against it, even all that is written in this book which Jeremiah hath prophesied against all the nations. (14) For many nations and great kings shall serve themselves of them also: and I will recompense them according to their deeds, and according to the works of their own hands. (15) For thus saith the LORD God of Israel unto me; Take the wine cup of this fury at my hand, and cause all the nations, to whom I send thee, to drink it. (16) And they shall drink, and be moved, and be mad, because of the sword that I will send among them. (17) Then took*

I the cup at the LORD's hand, and made all the nations to drink, unto whom the LORD had sent me.

In spite of the many helpful uses of the computer we have at our fingertips, there will always be those people who will exploit something intended to be used for good for their own selfish purposes. One of the evil uses of the computer is the promotion of witchcraft, namely, the telling of fortunes. The nature of man cannot change, unless that change comes from God and a willing heart.

Encoded within these following Scriptures are prophetical insights, enriched with words and phrases alluding to a time far into the future from Jeremiah's perspective. I feel it is important to paint a clearer picture of the day in which we are living.

Jeremiah 38:1-3. (1) *Then Shaphatiah the son of Mattan, and Gedaliah the son of Pashur, and Jucal the son of Shelemiah, and Pashur the son of Malchiah, heard the words that Jeremiah had spoken unto all the people, saying,* (2) *Thus saith the LORD, He that remaineth in this city shall die by the sword, by the famine, and by the pestilence: but he that goeth forth to the Chaldeans shall live; for he shall have his life for a prey, and shall live.* (3) *Thus saith the LORD, This city shall surely be given into the hand of the king of Babylon's army, which shall take it.*

1 וישמע שפטיה בן מתן וגדליהו בן־פשחור ויוכל בן־
שלמיהו ופשחור בן־מלכיה את־הדברים אשר ירמידו
מדבר אל־כל־העם לאמר: 2 כי אמר יהוה הישב בעיר
הזאת ימות בחרב ברעב ובדבר והיצא אל־הכשדים

יחיה והיתה־לו נפשו לשלל וחי: 3 כה אמר יהוה

הנתן תנתן העיר הזאת ביד חיל מלך־בבל ולכדה:

These prophecies were fulfilled exactly as the Lord had told Jeremiah. However, they allude to another scenario that is being fulfilled at this very moment.

Jeremiah 38:1. Starting with the first letter in the 18th word, counting forward every 41st letter spells *evil computer; machaiv avonnah;* מחשב עוננה. Avonnah also means *fortune telling*. The adjacent letters with the same ELS spell *Babylon*.

Though on many occasions the nation of Israel was in predicaments, seemingly without any solution, God was always faithful to answer them when they called upon Him. The same is true in our lives.

Jeremiah 38:2. Starting with the fourth letter in the sixth word, counting in reverse every 43rd letter spells *Teshuah;* תשועה. This word means *salvation (deliverance) from God by a Man.* We understand by the Holy Scriptures that in order for us to have salvation and deliverance, it must come from God through the Messiah.

Jeremiah 38:10. Starting with the first letter in the sixth word, counting forward every 38th letter spells *the Messiah;* המשיח. Adjacent letters at the same ELS spell *Your wonderful goodness; tovekah ye'peliah;* טובך יפליא.

THE MEANS OF COMMUNICATION

Communication was once house to house; field to field;

95

city to city; nation to nation. Today, there are many ways to communicate. For thousands of years, it was impossible for anyone to have instant contact with someone else in a distant land. What took weeks or months in the pre-modern era only takes seconds by our present-day means of communication. At one time the most rapid means was by courier of man or pigeon; then came the telegraph system; the next giant step was the telephone.

Today, it is possible to send a message to anyone in the world by choosing from six different sources of modern technology. All modern telecommunications are controlled by a power grid of electricity in some form—telephones, fax machines, telegraph, radio, television, and the Internet. This interweaves us throughout an awesome web of instant information and communication that is unprecedented. It is our generation that will see the climax of this age and the introduction into the Messianic kingdom. Perhaps the prophet had us in mind when he wrote: *Woe unto them that join house to house, that lay field to field, till there be no place, that they may be placed alone in the midst of the earth!* (Isaiah 5:8).

The prophet was giving us a picture of the end of time when everyone in this world will be interconnected one way or another. There is nothing wrong with close relationships that are godly, but when those relationships have evil intentions, then it is very wrong and ungodly.

These modern inventions were designed to benefit all mankind; however, some people are using them for evil purposes. If it were not for the Good News—the Gospel—for which many people are using these lightning-fast systems of communication, the Lord may have put an end to them long ago. It is the Holy Spirit-ordained use of these inventions, especially the computer and satellite ministries throughout the world, that are holding back the wrath of God on an ungodly world.

Isaiah 5:16-19. (16) *But the LORD of hosts shall be exalted in judgment, and God that is holy shall be sanctified in righteousness. (17) Then shall the lambs feed after their manner, and the waste places of the fat ones shall strangers eat. (18) Woe unto them that draw iniquity with cords of vanity, and sin as it were with a cart rope. (19) That say, Let him make speed, and hasten his work, that we may see it: and let the counsel of the Holy One of Israel draw nigh and come, that we many know it!*

16 ויגבה יהוה צבאות במשפט והאל הקדוש נקדש בצדקה:

17 ורעו כבשים כדברם וחרבות מחים גרים יאכלו:

18 הוי משכי העון בחבלי השוא וכעבות העגלה חטאה:

19 האמרים ימהר יחישה מעשהו למען נראה ותקרב

ותבואה עצת קדוש ישראל ונדעה:

Isaiah 5:18. Starting with the first letter in the second word, counting in reverse every 21st letter spells *computer; machaiv;* מחשב. In the same ELS-count of 21 we find *the adversary; haSatan;* השטן.

Isaiah 5:19. Starting with the fifth letter in the third word, counting in reverse every 17th letter spells *the satellite; ha'til;* הטיל.

Isaiah 5:20. *Woe unto them that call evil good, and good evil; that put darkness for light, and light for darkness; that put bitter for sweet, and sweet for bitter!*

We can readily understand by these insights that there is a foul spirit controlling the secular media's exchange of information that is now available for everyone. Remember, Satan is the prince and power of the air; nevertheless, we can use these same inventions for the glory of God and overcome Satan and his cohorts. In the midst of trouble, the Lord is always available to save and rescue His people. Below are a few encoded insights that are quite refreshing.

Isaiah 5:19. Starting with the third letter in the ninth word, counting every 11th letter in reverse spells *hope; tikvah;* תקוה. The adjacent letters at the same ELS spell *Savior; Moshiah;* מושעה. Also, the name of the Messiah is encoded at the same ELS.

God is the only hope we have in this world or the world to come. He is our Savior and always ready to save upon request. Regardless of who you are, one day you and I will have to stand in His presence and give an answer to Him for our lives. If you decide to follow Him, you will be eternally blessed by His presence. But if you reject Him, you will be separated from Him forever. God has something new and refreshing for all who receive His prophetic promise of the New Covenant that is available at this very moment. Please read what Jeremiah prophesied concerning this promise.

Jeremiah 31:31-34. (31) *Behold, the days come, saith the LORD, that I will make a new covenant with the house of Israel, and with the house of Judah:* (32) *Not according to the covenant that I made with their fathers in the day that I took them by the* *hand to bring them out of the land of Egypt; which my covenant they brake, although I was a husband unto them, saith the LORD: (33) But this shall be the covenant that I will make with the house of Israel; After those days, saith the LORD, I will put my law in their inward parts, and write it in their hearts; and will be their God, and they shall be my people. (34) And they shall teach no more every man his neighbor, and every man his brother, saying, Know the LORD: for they shall all know me, from the least of them unto the greatest of them, saith the LORD: for I will forgive their iniquity, and I will remember their sin no more.*

These were prophecies concerning the New Covenant that God Himself would make with Israel and anyone who would call upon Him. There has only been one New Covenant made since the Torah was written 3,500 years ago, which I will give details about in the upcoming chapters.

Four

THE NAME
OF THE MESSIAH

Tom here have been many arguments surrounding the man called Jesus Christ. The questions that have been asked since the first century are answerable by responsible witnesses and testimonies of famous scholars—Jewish and Gentile alike. The ultimate question is: Was Jesus the Messiah? Are there archeological and scientific evidences to back up the faith of untold millions of people who have believed that He was, and is, the Lord and Savior of the whole world?

With the proliferation of misinformation that has flooded some religious societies since the first century A.D., it is often very difficult to know how to discern truth from fiction. Traditions of men have obscured the truth of secular history concerning Jesus the Christ. Shamelessly, some unbelievers disgrace His name, but when so-called Christians, who should know better, try to discredit that wonderful name of Jesus, it hinges on absolute blasphemy and heresy.

I would set forth some of these truths from secular history.

PILATE'S REPORT

In 1887, Rev. W. D. Mahan published a book titled *The Archko Volume*. His comprehensive and worldwide research for documentation from the first century took him to the Vatican in Rome, Italy and to Constantinople, Turkey. Among many other treasured writings, he located a letter written on a papyrus scroll to Caesar by Pontius Pilate dated about 31 A.D., following the crucifixion of Jesus Christ. Below is a testimony given by Pontius Pilate on this very delicate matter.

The Archko Volume, pages 13-14

> With this correspondence I received the following document, and I must confess that, although it is not inspired, yet the words burned in my heart as the words of Christ in the hearts of his disciples, and I am satisfied from the spirit it breathes that it must be true. I am aware that though the Jews were in subjection to the Romans, yet they still held their ecclesiastical authority, and the Romans not only submitted to their decisions, but executed their decrees on their subjects. Knowing there was not such a piece of history to be found in all the world, and being deeply interested myself, as also, hundreds of others to whom I have read it, I have concluded to give it to the public.

> Upon getting hold of this report of Pilate, I commenced to investigate this subject, and after many years of trial and the expenditure of considerable

money, I found that there were many of such records still preserved at the Vatican in Rome and at Constantinople, that had been carried there by the Emperor of Rome about the middle of the third century. I therefore procured the necessary assistance, and on September 21, 1883, I set sail for those foreign lands to make the investigation in person.

Believing that no event of such importance to the world as the death of Jesus of Nazareth could have transpired without some record being made of it by his enemies in their courts, legislations, and histories, I commenced investigating the subject. After many years of study, and after consulting various histories and corresponding with many scholars, I received the assistance of two learned men, Drs. McIntosh and Twyman, and went to the Vatican at Rome, and then to the Jewish Talmuds of Constantinople. As a result I have compiled this book, which will be found one of the most strange and interesting books ever read. It may appear fragmentary, but the reader must remember that it is the record of men made nearly two thousand years ago.

Excerpts from Pontius Pilate's letter written to Caesar

Pilate's description of Jesus, page 131

Among the various rumors that came to my ears there was one in particular that attracted my attention.

A young man, it was said, had appeared in Galilee preaching with a noble unction a new law in the name of the God that had sent him. At first I was apprehensive that his design was to stir up the people against the Romans, but my fears were soon dispelled. Jesus of Nazareth spoke rather as friend of the Romans than of the Jews. One day in passing by the place of Siloe, where there was a great concourse of people, I observed in the midst of the group a young man who was leaning against a tree, calmly addressing the multitude. I was told it was Jesus. This I could easily have suspected, so great was the difference between him and those listening to him. His golden-colored hair and beard gave to his appearance a celestial aspect. He appeared to be about thirty years of age. Never have I seen a sweeter or more serene countenance.

Pilate's first meeting with Jesus, pages 133-134

I wrote to Jesus requesting an interview with him at the praetorium. He came. You know that in my veins flows the Spanish mixed with Roman blood—as incapable of fear as it is of weak emotion. When the Nazarene made his appearance, I was walking in my basilic, and my feet seemed fastened with an iron hand to the marble pavement, and I trembled in every limb as does a guilty culprit, though the Nazarene was as calm as innocence itself. When he came up to me he stopped, and by a signal sign he seemed to say to me, "I am here," though he spoke not a word. For some time I contemplated with admiration and awe this extraordinary type of man—a type of man unknown to our numerous painters, who have given form and figure to all the gods and the heroes. There was nothing about him that was repelling in its character, yet I felt too awed and tremulous to approach him.

Pilate describes the mob at the crucifixion, page 141

Often in our civil commotions have I witnessed the furious anger of the multitude, but nothing could be compared to what I witnessed on this occasion. It might have been truly said that all the phantoms of the infernal regions had assembled at Jerusalem. The crowd appeared not to walk, but to be borne off and whirled as a vortex, rolling along in living waves from the portals of the praetorium even unto Mount Zion, with howling screams, shrieks, and vociferations such as were never heard in the seditions of the Pannonia, or in the tumults of the forum.

Pilate describes great noise and darkness at Golgotha, page 142

A loud clamor was heard proceeding from Golgotha, which, borne on the winds, seemed to announce an agony such as was never heard by mortal ears. Dark clouds lowered over the pinnacle of the temple, and setting over the city covered it with a veil. So dreadful

THE NAME OF THE MESSIAH

were the signs that men saw both in the heavens and on the earth that Dionysius the Aeropagite is reported to have exclaimed, "Either the author of nature is suffering or the universe is falling apart."

Pilate quoting Ben Isham, a sentry at the tomb, page 145

He said that at about the beginning of the fourth watch they saw a soft and beautiful light over the sepulchre. He at first thought that the women had come to embalm the body of Jesus, as was their custom, but he could not see how they had gotten through the guards. While these thoughts were passing through his mind, behold, the whole place was lighted up, and there seemed to be crowds of the dead in their graveclothes. All seemed to be shouting and filled with ecstasy, while all around and above was the most beautiful music he had ever heard; and the whole air seemed to be full of voices praising God.

Pilate's concluding remarks in his report, page 147

I am almost ready to say, as did Manlius at the cross, "Truly this was the Son of God."

NEW TESTAMENT ACROSTIC?

Among all the spiritual and scientific approaches to the phenomenal Bible codes that I have ever read, Dr. Chuck Missler has developed one of the most remarkable. With his permission, I quote the following:

In the New Testament there also appears to be a possible Hebrew acrostic that generally goes unnoticed.

When Jesus was crucified, Pilate wrote the formal epitaph that was nailed to the cross. The particular wording he chose displeased the Jewish leadership, and they asked him to change it. He refused. There are some interesting aspects to this incident that are not apparent in our English translations of John 19:19-22.

"And Pilate wrote a title, and put it on the cross. And the writing was, JESUS OF NAZARETH THE KING OF THE JEWS. This title then read many of the Jews: for the place where Jesus was crucified was nigh to the city: and it was written in Hebrew, and Greek, and Latin. Then said the chief priests of the Jews to Pilate, Write not, The King of the Jews; but that he said, I am the King of the Jews. Pilate answered, What I have written I have written."

The chief priest's distress highlights something we might otherwise miss. Notice that Pilate refused to revise the epitaph he had composed. This may have more significance than is apparent in our English translations. The Hebrew is shown below (remember, Hebrew goes from right to left):

ישוע הנצרי ומלך היהודים

HaYehudim W'Melech HaNazarei Yeshua
Jesus the Nazarene and King of the Jews.

What we don't notice in the English translation is the potential acrostic made up of the first letter of each word, which gives us the initials, YHWH, *Yahweh*: יהוה. [Special note: *The vav (ו) in the Hebrew can give us the same sound as the* (w) *in English.* Therefore, for the sake of clarity, I used the English form in the transliteration instead of the Hebrew transliteration.]

If Pilate had rewritten it in the manner they had requested him to, it would not have spelled out the name of God. Did Pilate realize this? Was it deliberate? If so, did he do it just to upset the Jewish leadership, which he realized had delivered Him up for envy? Or was he beginning to suspect that there was more going on here than he previously realized?

It is interesting that Jesus' enemies recalled that He promised to rise on the third day. When they later requested a special guard for the tomb, Pilate also responded with an enigmatic remark, "Make it as sure as you can." What did he mean by that? Had he begun to suspect that Jesus really was who He said He was? Was Pilate really surprised when Jesus was resurrected after three days? One wonders.[5]

NAPOLEON BONAPARTE

One of the potential world conquerors, Napoleon

---

[5]Chuck Missler, *Cosmic Codes* (Coeur d'Alene: Koinonia House, 1999), pp. 86-88. Used by permission.

Bonaparte, faded away like so many other great men of their time. But before his death in 1821, he gave a dissertation concerning the man called Jesus Christ.

Did Napoleon really receive a revelation from God while standing in the Great Pyramid? While this may be debated, we do know that Napoleon seemed resigned to the outcome of the Battle of Waterloo even before it began, and his final defeat in this battle had often been regarded as an act of God. Napoleon was a would-be world ruler who lived before his time, because the preordained time for the final Gentile ruler of earth had not arrived. The great general himself seemed to realize this, and he realized also that Jesus Christ was God's anointed King of kings as reflected in his dissertations during his last days on St. Helena. *Halley's Bible Handbook* reports Napoleon as saying:

"Alexander, Caesar, Charlemagne and myself founded empires; but upon what? Force. Jesus founded his empire on Love; and at this hour millions would die for him. I myself have inspired multitudes with such affection that they would die for me. But my presence was necessary. Now that I am in St. Helena, where are my friends? I am forgotten, soon to return to the earth, and become food for worms. What an abyss between my misery and the eternal kingdom of Christ, who is proclaimed, loved, adored, and which is extending over all the earth. Is this death? I tell you, the death of Christ is the death of a God. I tell you, *Jesus Christ is God*."[6]

Please notice that one statement stands out above the others. Napoleon said that Jesus Christ *is* God. He did *not* say He *was* God. Apparently, Napoleon had a revelation concerning Jesus. I do not know if he ever received Him as his Lord and Savior, but logic would tell you he was not far from the kingdom of God.

ARCHEOLOGICAL EVIDENCE ABOUT JESUS

There is archeological evidence from the first century that the Hebrew name of Jesus, *Yeshua;* ישוע is spelled in this manner. This is material I have personally researched.

In the spring of 1873, Effendi Abu Saud, while constructing his house on the eastern slopes of the Mount of Olives near the road to ancient Bethany, accidentally discovered a cave that proved to be an ancient burial catacomb. Inside, he found thirty ancient stone coffins. Professor Charles Claremont-Gannueau examined the ossuaries in this ancient family sepulchral cave carved out of limestone rock. The Jews in the first century buried their dead either in the ground or in a tomb. Several years later they would clean the bones of the

---

[6]Dr. David Webber and N. W. Hutchings, *New Light on the Great Pyramid* (Oklahoma City: Hearthstone Publishing), 71-72.

skeleton and re-bury these bones in a small limestone ossuary, often forty-five inches long, twenty inches wide, and twenty-five inches high. The lids of these ossuaries are triangular, semi-circular, or rectangular. Inscriptions containing the name and identification of the deceased were painted or engraved on the sides or on the lids of the ossuaries in Hebrew or Greek. Claremont-Gannueau was excited to note that several ossuaries were inscribed with crosses or the name *Jesus;* ישוע, proving that these Jewish deceased were Christians.

Engraved on the sides of three of these ossuaries from this cave were the names of *Eleazar;* אלעזר (the Hebrew form of the Greek name Lazarus), Martha, and Mary. Those names were followed by the sign of the cross, proving they were Christian. In the Gospel of John we read the touching story of Christ raising His friend Lazarus from the dead. "Now a certain man was sick, Lazarus of Bethany, the town of Mary and her sister Martha" (John 11:1). Claremont-Gannueau noted that this was one of the most important archeological discoveries ever made concerning the origins of the early New Testament Church. He wrote, "This catacomb on the Mount of Olives belonged apparently to one of the earliest families which joined the new religion of Christianity. In this group of sarcophagi, some of which have the Christian symbol and some have not, we are, so to speak, (witnessing the) actual unfolding of Christianity. Personally, I think that many of the Hebrew-speaking people whose remains are contained in these ossuaries were among the first followers of Christ....The appearance of Christianity at the very gates of Jerusalem is, in my opinion, extraordinary and unprecedented. Somehow the new [Christian] doctrine must have made its way into the Jewish system....The association of the sign of the cross with (the name of *Jesus;* ישוע) written in Hebrew alone constitutes a valuable fact."[7]

THE FEASTS OF THE LORD AND THEIR PURPOSE

In reference to the New Covenant and the crucifixion, I must go back to third chapter of Genesis and begin with the first, and major, Messianic prophecy concerning the coming Deliverer in regards to the fall in the Garden of Eden. Man had sinned and was eternally separated from God, but the Lord in His compassion had mercy on Adam and Eve and gave them a promise that He would save them from their sins. The phrase, *the Messiah*, with His name, are both encoded within this area and refer to the coming Deliverer.

This verse is the pivotal point for all the Feasts of the Lord. However, the Feasts were not introduced to Israel until many years later, when there was a need and the circumstances were suitable for demonstrating their true meaning. All the Feasts

---

[7]Yacov Rambsel, *His Name Is Jesus: The Mysterious Yeshua Codes* (Toronto: Frontier Research Publications, 1997), pp. 92-94.

were there in the beginning as types, but only as a rehearsal for the ultimate fulfillment, which foreshadowed events hundreds of years into the future. This process of foreshadowed events began to be played out about 3,500 years ago, particularly when the first Passover was held in Egypt as a great Messianic lesson of the coming Redeemer, the Lamb of God.

Genesis 3:15. *And I will put enmity between thee and the woman, and between thy seed and her seed; it [He] shall bruise thy head, and thou [serpent] shalt bruise his heel.*

Genesis 3:15. Starting with the third letter in the second word, counting in reverse every 69th letter spells *Jesus; Yeshua;* ישוע. The adjacent letters at the same ELS spells *atonement for all; kippur ki'kol;* כפר ככל.

Within these Scriptures is encoded the *method* by which the Seed of the woman would bring salvation to a sin-filled world—also, *how* this would be accomplished.

Genesis 3:12. Starting with the third letter in the 11th word, counting in reverse every 46th letter spells *crucify; tzalab;* צלב. This also means *a cross.* The adjacent letters at the same ELS spell *the lamb; haseh;* השה.

When God saw the fig leaf-covering made by Adam and Eve, He knew that this was not sufficient to atone for their sin. So He sacrificed an innocent animal, using its skin to cover Adam and Eve. This gives us a detailed picture of when God would complete our salvation by the shedding of the blood of the Lamb of God. These insights give us a preview of an event that would take place in God's appointed time. The Lamb of God would be crucified for the sins of the whole world.

Genesis 3:7. Starting with the seventh letter in the first word, counting forward every 20th letter spells *the Messiah; haMashiach;* המשיח. The adjacent letters at the same ELS spell *dedication; chanukah;* חנכה. Later in the history of Israel, this word became what is called *the Feast of Dedication (Lights).* These insights tell us that the Messiah will be completely and compassionately dedicated to fulfilling the deliverance of fallen man by bringing forth the heavenly light—Himself.

Hidden somewhere within the Hebrew text are all the promises of God. These Scriptures reverberate with the culmination of those promises. The Word of God has enormous depth that has yet to be explored. However, in these last days He has broken the seal that has hidden these precious jewels in His Word.

Genesis 3:16. Starting with the second letter in the third word, counting in reverse every 36th letter spells *freewill offering; minchah;* מנחה. This is a sacrificial offering unto the Lord, and it must be given by one's own volition. Certainly, this is a picture of the greater sacrificial offering that would be made by the willing Lamb of God at the appointed time. This offering can be an afternoon prayer, a meat offering, or an oblation unto the Lord. But most commonly, it is a sacrificial offering of a lamb.

Genesis 3:14. Starting with the second letter in the second word, counting forward every 23rd letter spells *the sin (guilt) offering; ha'ash'mah;* האשמה.

This same word is used in Isaiah 53:10. *Yet it pleased the LORD to bruise him; he hath put him to grief: when thou shalt make his soul an offering for sin* [אשם]. This word also means *to make desolate; to destroy; to punish; to put to open shame.*

Genesis 3:13. Starting with the second letter in the eighth word, counting forward every 30th letter spells *praises of the Lamb; tehillat haseh*; תהלת השה.

Genesis 3:8. Starting with the first letter in the 15th word, counting forward every 30th letter spells *the song of love; ohavah le'shir*; אהבה לשיר. Adjacent letters at the same ELS spell *behold God; haElohim*; הא אלהים.

What God is showing us with these insights is that He loved Adam and Eve. The Lamb of God would be not only *their* substitute, but also that for *all* people everywhere. In the course of time and at God's appointed season, the sin offering would be made for the whole world. Then the redeemed of the Lord can praise Him and sing unto the Lamb the songs of praise and love. *And they sung a new song, saying, Thou art worthy to take the book, and to open the seals thereof: for thou wast slain, and hast redeemed us to God by thy blood out of every kindred, and tongue, and people, and nation* (Revelation 5:9).

Many years after Adam and Eve were banished from the Garden of Eden, the Lord continually kept His hand on the royal bloodline to insure that their Messiah would be born thousands of years into the future. At times, it seemed that His plan would be thwarted by the enemy, but God in His sovereignty brought His divine plan to completion at the proper time in history. He intro-duced Israel to the Seven Feasts, which would project His divine calendar into the appropriate time and place for their fulfillment.

When the children of Israel were being held in cruel bondage by the Egyptians, God heard their cries and had com-passion on them. He sent them a man named Moses to deliver them from oppression and bring them out from under the iron fist of the Pharaoh. The task seemed insurmountable, but God had put in motion another part of His plan to reveal His grace and love to the whole human race. Here again, the Lord used a model to express the ultimate meaning of the archetype, the lamb. The Lord was ready to introduce the whole house of Israel to the first Feast of the Lord, *the Passover;* הפסח. The Hebrew word for *Feast* means *appointment, moaid;* מועד. In other words, it is *an appointment of the Lord.*

The record of the first Passover came on the eve of the tenth pestilence when God was dealing with the Egyptians for the release of the house of Israel from bondage. God instructed Moses to have every household sacrifice an innocent lamb between the evening on the 14th of Nisan. This would be at 3:00 P. M., which was at least three hours before the 15th of Nisan. They were to take the blood of the lamb and put it on the lintel and the doorposts of each dwelling where they we going to eat the Passover meal. Everyone was wel-comed to participate, even the Egyptians. However, since this would be the last plague before they left Egypt, God was giving us an eternal lesson on the power of the blood when properly applied.

Exodus 12:3-8. (3) *Speak ye unto all the congregation of Israel, saying, In the tenth day of this month they shall take to them every man a lamb, according to the house of their fathers, a lamb for a house: (4) And if the household be too little for the lamb, let him and his neighbor next unto his house take it according to the number of the souls; every man according to his eating shall make your count for the lamb. (5) Your lamb shall be without blemish, a male of the first year: ye shall take it out from the sheep, or from the goats: (6) And ye shall keep it up until the fourteenth day of the same month: and the whole assembly of the congregation of Israel shall kill it in the evening. (7) And they shall take of the* blood, *and strike it on the two side posts and on the upper door post of the houses, wherein they shall eat it. (8) And they shall eat the flesh in that night, roast with fire, and unleavened bread; and with bitter herbs they shall eat it.*

There are at least five things about this first Passover that stand out in my mind. First, it had to be a lamb without blemish. Second, it had to be a one-year-old male. Third, they had to kill the lamb at 3:00 P. M. and gather its blood. Fourth, they had to apply the blood of the lamb on their dwelling places. Fifth, they had to eat the Passover lamb inside the house and not go out until morning. They had to be totally committed in their participation of this Feast.

The Lord told Moses that He would pass over the houses that were covered with the blood of the lamb. But regarding the houses that did not have the blood covering, the plague of death would take their firstborn of man and animal.

Exodus 12:23. *For the LORD will pass through to smite the Egyptians; and when he seeth the blood upon the lintel, and on the two side posts, the LORD will pass over the door, and will not suffer the destroyer to come in unto your houses to smite you.*

Reflecting upon these previous verses, I cannot feel anything other than a deep sense of awe and humility about the divine manifestation of this tenth plague, which had to do with life, blood, and death. It was a demonstration of life for those who sacrificed the lamb and applied its blood, but it was a curse upon those who ignored the commandment. This first Passover was a rehearsal for the Great Passover when the Lamb of God would give His life; however, in order to receive life, one must be covered with the precious blood of the Lamb. *For without the shedding of blood there is no remission of sin.*

Since the first Passover lamb was a prophetic picture of the final fulfillment of this Feast, additional information concerning the sacrifice of Jesus, the Lamb of God, is meticulously encoded throughout Exodus 12.

Exodus 12:29. *And it came to pass, that at midnight the LORD smote all the first-born in the land of Egypt, from the first-born of Pharaoh that sat on his throne unto the first-born of the captive that was in the dungeon; and all the first-born of cattle.*

Exodus 12:29. Starting with the third letter in the fourth word, counting in reverse every 37th letter spells *the cross; ha't-salav;* הצלב. The adjacent letters at the same ELS spell *for Jesus; kiYeshua;* כישוע.

This gives us the precise method that would be used to finalize and fulfill the meaning of the Passover. Please take special notice of the following details from the cross of Jesus. His blood was at the top of the wooden cross from His head wounds; the sides of the cross were filled with blood from His pierced hands; the foot of the cross was saturated with the blood from nail-pierced feet. The first Passover lamb and the application of its blood upon the doorpost and lintel painted a perfect picture of the Lamb of God who would shed His blood in the same basic manner.

When the last plague was put into effect, it destroyed the flower of Egypt and the Pharaoh as well. The Egyptians were in hot pursuit of Moses and the house of Israel when they were drowned in the Red Sea. Many times we forget that there were eleven plagues, not ten, that took there toll upon the empire that held God's people in slavery. Not only did God destroy the Egyptians, but their gods as well.

Psalm 136:12-15. (12) *With a strong hand, and with a stretched out arm: for his mercy endureth for ever.* (13) *To him which divided the Red Sea into parts; for his mercy endureth for ever:* (14) *And made Israel to pass through the midst of it: for his mercy endureth for ever:* (15) *but overthrew Pharaoh and his host in the Red Sea: for his mercy endureth for ever.*

It wasn't until forty years later that the children of Israel entered the promised land. This is where they were to fully keep the 613 commandments of the Torah. The additional six Feasts of the Lord were given to them while in the desert, but they could not completely fulfill all the commandments and the Feasts until the Temple was built about five hundred years later. Most of the 613 commandments have to do with the Temple service and worship. Israel, before the Temple was built, was in training for the time when they could fully exercise the meaning of all the commandments and point us to the final meaning of each of the Feasts of the Lord.

Many years later King David wrote the prophetic Psalm 22, describing in great detail the manner in which the Messiah would be put to death and the hateful persecutors of that event. It also contains phrases the Messiah would say while hanging on the cross (tree).

Psalm 22:1. *My God, my God, why hast thou forsaken me?*

אלי אלי למה עזבתני

ali ali lamah ahzabtani

The seven statements that Jesus made during the six hours He was on the cross are recorded in the four Gospels of the New Testament. Of these seven sayings, the phrase, "*My God, my God, why have you forsaken me?*" is recorded in Matthew and Mark. It is so important for us to understand that the very prophetic statement that David wrote in Psalm 22 would be repeated and fulfilled to the letter by the person about whom the Psalmist was referring.

Matthew 27:46. *And about the ninth hour Jesus cried with a loud voice, saying, Eli, Eli, lama sa-bach'tha-ni? that is to say, My God, My God, why hast thou forsaken me?*

There are many prophecies and encoded insights within Psalm 22, but I want to bring your attention to two of them that are very outstanding.

Psalm 22:16. *For dogs have compassed me: the assembly of the wicked have inclosed me: they pierced my hands and my feet.*

כי־סבבוני כלבים עדת מרעים הקיפוני כארי ידי ורגלי:

Psalm 22:16. Starting with the third letter in the fifth word, counting in reverse every 26th letter spells *the sign for Jesus; aot ki'Yeshua;* אות כישוע.

What sign was the Lord referring to here? It could only be the sign of crucifixion on a tree with the piercing of the hands and feet.

I had a statistical analysis made on this insight and the results were staggering. For this code to happen by chance the odds are .00006 to one million. In other words, it would be impossible for this to be imbedded within this text by man. It had to be put there by God Himself, confirming the heavenly and supernatural source of the Word of God.

The first mention of hanging on a tree is in Genesis 40:19, where the butler was crucified by Pharaoh, though nails were never used in the crucifixions in Egypt. This was later introduced in Rome and the provinces under the Caesar. Strangely enough, the name of *Jesus; Yeshua;* ישׁוע is encoded at 17-ELS within this text. The crucifixion was later developed by the Romans as a means of punishing by a cruel death any perpetrator whose crime was against the laws of Rome or the co-rulers of an occupied country.

This next portion of information is so awesome and mind-boggling that it is very difficult to explain the uniqueness of it with my finite mind. For many years the rabbis taught that Psalm 22 and other prophecies referring to the same subject *did not have any connection whatsoever* with the man called Jesus the Messiah. They were so bent on protecting their views that the truth of this was never truly proven, even though many of the Rabbis for many centuries understood the coding system in the Bible. These are some of the reasons I was prompted by the Holy Spirit to do a scientific analysis in these Messianic prophecies and reveal the true name of the Messiah, *Jesus; Yeshua;* ישוע.

Psalm 22:12. Starting with the second letter in the eighth word, counting in reverse every 45th letter spells *Jesus my Christ; Yeshua Mashiachi;* ישוע משיחי.

An analysis was made on this encoded insight, and the results were even more staggering than the previous one mentioned. For this to happen by chance, within the 1,012 letters of Psalm 22, the odds came out to be .000000000000 to one million. *Notice, these are no odds.* It would be absolutely out of the range of any natural mind to have encrypted this insight other than that of the Lord God.

According to the mathematical analysis, it is absolutely impossible for it to have been encoded within this text. So I suggested an analysis on the whole book of Psalms, which contains 78,832 letters. The results were the same. At this point I was so exhilarated that it was difficult for me to contain my dignity. I asked if an analysis could be done on the whole Bible—1,196,922 letters—and again, I was shocked into a deep wonder at the Word of God. I could never, ever in my whole lifetime have any doubts as to the author and ownership of the Holy Bible. It is my Lord God. Psalm 22 is the only place in all the Bible where the combination with this count is encoded. This phenomenon occurs several times with other encoded insights throughout the Bible. This proves from a scientific standpoint that God was in complete control of the total writings of the Holy Bible.

My main thought on this after I came down from the heights of glory is that He is my personal Messiah. That means that I would have to know Him personally for Him to be mine. Yes, this is true. In 1941 I met Him at the age of eleven, when I invited Him into my heart. He then became my personal Savior when I received Him as my Lord God and precious Redeemer.

After Jesus had been executed and buried in the tomb, He remained there for three days and three nights. Then, on the third day He resurrected from the dead and was seen by many for forty days before He ascended into heaven. The disciple Thomas was absent when Jesus appeared to some of the disciples. He said that he would not believe unless he could see the nailprints in His hands and touch His side—the signs of the cross. Well, our compassionate Lord heard Thomas and appeared unto him as He had the others.

John 20:26-28. (26) *And after eight days again his disciples were within, and Thomas with them: then came Jesus, the doors being shut, and stood in the midst, and said, Peace be unto you.* (27) *Then saith he to Thomas, Reach hither thy finger, and behold* *my hands; and reach hither thy hand, and thrust it into my side: and be not faithless, but believing.* (28) *And Thomas answered and said unto him, My Lord and my God.*

This is a very bold statement coming from a Jewish man who was raised in the tradition of the Torah. For Thomas to call Jesus his Lord and his God, he would certainly have had a revelation of who Jesus really was. With that revelation, he pronounced Jesus to be his God and his Lord. What I am referring to in this testimony of Thomas is that we must believe that He is the Lord of glory and the God of creation and our substitute, or else we fall short of a personal relationship with Him.

From Psalm 22, I would like to elaborate on some dynamic insights depicting many things that were done to Jesus during the grueling hours leading up to His death on the cross.

Psalm 22:14-15. (14) *I am poured out like water, and all my bones are out of joint: my heart is like wax; it is melted in the midst of my bowels.* (15) *My strength is dried up like a potsherd; and my tongue cleaveth to my jaws; and thou hast brought me into the dust of death.*

14 כמים נשפכתי והתפרדו כל־עצמותי היה לבי כדונג נמס בתוך מעי:

15 יבש כחרש כחי ולשוני מדבק מלקוחי ולעפר־מוה תשפתני:

Psalm 22:15. Starting with the first letter in the sixth word, counting forward every ninth letter spells *Behold Messiah; hain'Mashiach;* הן משיח.

The writer of Psalm 22 is describing in detail a horrible death by crucifixion. Every facet of the prophecy was fulfilled by the Messiah on that wonderful, but infamous, day. Wonderful, I say, because He paid the ultimate price for my redemption, but infamous because of the total degradation He suffered for all the sins in the world for all time.

Psalm 22:6-7. (6) *But I am a worm, and no man; a reproach of men, and despised of the people.* (7) *All they that see me laugh me to scorn: they shoot out the lip, they shake the head.*

ואנכי תולעת ולא־איש חרפת אדם ובזוי־עם:

כל־ראי ילענו לי יפטירו בשפה יניעו ראש:

Psalm 22:7. Starting with the fifth letter in the first word, counting forward every 11th letter spells *Jesus in silence; Yeshua be'sheli;* ישוע בשלי.

These insights add more information about who the Psalmist was speaking of, confirming again the awesomeness of the supernatural Word of God. *Behold Messiah* and *Jesus in silence.* Compare these to Matthew 27:39. *And they that passed by reviled him, wagging their heads.* Or consider Mark 15:3-5. (3) *And the chief priests accused him of many things: but he answered nothing.* (4) *And Pilate asked him again, saying, Answerest thou nothing? behold how many things they witness against thee.* (5) *But Jesus yet answered nothing; so that Pilate marveled.*

Another Psalm that has profound predictions concerning the crucifixion was also written by David. The Spirit of God was upon David to write many prophecies about the death, burial, and resurrection of Jesus. So detailed are these that it would be impossible for them to be fulfilled by accident. We must conclude that the Lord Himself was instrumental in accomplishing every jot and tittle of His Word.

Psalm 69:19-21. (19) *Thou hast known my reproach, and my shame, and my dishonor: mine adversaries are all before thee. (20) Reproach hath broken my heart; and I am full of heaviness: and I looked for some to take pity, but there was none; and for comforters, but I found none. (21) They gave me also gall for my meat; and in my thirst they gave me vinegar to drink.*

There are at least four prophecies within these verses that were fulfilled by Jesus when He was on the cross. If He would have been just a man, He could not have caused these to be fulfilled. But because He is God manifested in the flesh, every letter and word of His shall be accomplished according the His will.

1. They blasphemed Him (put Him to open shame).

2. They gave Him vinegar to drink.

3. All have forsaken Him.

4. His heart was broken with sadness.

Hidden within this text is the name of the person the Psalmist was describing.

Psalm 69:21. Starting with the third letter in the eighth word, counting forward every 18th letter spells *blaspheme (jeer) Jesus; mock Yeshua;* מוק ישוע.

We see the fulfillment of these prophecies in detail as the Psalmist described them at least one thousand years before Jesus was crucified.

1. Matthew 27:31. *And after that they had mocked [jeered] him, they took the yoke off from him, and put his own raiment on him, and led him away to crucify him.*

2. Matthew 27:34. *They gave him vinegar to drink mingled with gall: and when he had tasted thereof, he would not drink.*

3. Matthew 26:56. *But all this was done, that the scriptures of the prophets might be fulfilled. Then all the disciples forsook him, and fled.*

4. John 19:34. *But one of the soldiers with a spear pierced his side, and forthwith came there out blood and water.* [The fact that blood and water came out from His pierced side proves, according to the physiologists, that He died from a saddened and broken heart.]

In Genesis chapter 1, God recorded information for us about the sin offering that would be given at the appropriate time. The Hebrew phrase used in this text is *God in the expanse; Elohim birkiah;* אלהים ברקיע. The name of Jesus is encoded twice from this phrase at 26-ELS. This is quite remarkable that His name would appear in this text. My thinking on this is that He is God of the expanse as well as all of creation.

Genesis 1:15. Starting with the fourth letter in the third word, counting forward every 26th letter spells *Jesus the sin offering; ashamot Yeshua;* אשמת ישוע. His name appears again in this text at 26-ELS.

God had made provisions for our sin offering prior to the advent in the Garden of Eden when Adam and Eve ate the forbidden fruit and sin entered into the world. For redemption to be complete, the Lamb of God would have to give His blood. For without the shedding of blood there is no remission of sins.

Genesis 2:6. Starting with the second letter in the fourth word, counting forward every tenth letter spells *declare the blood and of Jesus; na'um hadahm ve'Yeshua;* נאם הדם וישוע. Another way of saying this phrase is *declare Yeshua and the blood.*

The name of *Jesus; Yeshua;* ישוע appears twice in this same text at the ten-letter ELS. This is yet another phenomenon of the codes that sheds additional light on the importance of our atonement through the precious blood of the Lamb of God.

The adjacent letters at nine ELS spell *the song of the Lamb; shir haseh;* שיר השה. Also, the name *Moses;* משה is encoded in this same text.

These insights refer to the Old and New Testament saints who will be in heaven, singing the songs of glory and praise before the Lamb of God. *And they sing the song of Moses the servant of God, and the song of the Lamb, saying, Great and marvelous are thy works, Lord God Almighty; just and true are thy ways, thou King of saints* (Revelation 15:3). Moses represents the Old Covenant, and the Lamb represents the New Covenant.

Leviticus 17:11. *For the life of the flesh is in the blood: and I have given it to you upon the altar to make an atonement for your souls: for it is the blood that maketh an atonement for the soul.*

Hebrews 9:22-24. (22) *And almost all things are by the law [Torah] purged with blood; and without shedding of blood is no* *remission. (23) It was therefore necessary that the patterns of things in the heavens should be purified with these; but the heavenly things themselves with better sacrifices than these. (24) For Christ [Messiah] is not entered into the holy places made with hands, which are the figures of the true; but into heaven itself, now to appear in the presence of God for us.*

There is an additional encoded insight that I want to bring to your attention now that is related to the high priest's entering into the Holy of Holies with blood and for atonement.

Leviticus 21:10. *And he that is the high priest among his brethren, upon whose head the anointing oil was poured, and that is consecrated to put on the garments, shall not uncover his head, nor rend his clothes.*

והכהן הגדול מאחיו אשר־יוצק על־ראשו שמן המשחה ומלא

את־ידו ללבש את־הבגדים את־ראשו לא יפרע ובגדיו לא יפרם:

Leviticus 21:10. Starting with the second letter in the first word, counting forward every third letter spells *Behold, the blood of Jesus; hain dahm Yeshua;* הנ דם ישוע. The phrase, *my Messiah;* משיחי, is also encoded through this same text.

Encoded in this same area of Scripture is every animal that was used in the sacrifce for the various offerings. Each one of these represent the Lamb of God and the different types of offerings that would be made for the complete redemption of the whole world. There are at least twenty-eight different insights within this same area that are associated with the High Priest and His function. Jesus is the High Priest that took His own blood into the Holy of Holies in heaven for atonement for all who would call upon Him.

There were seven phrases that Jesus said while hanging on the cross at Golgatha (Calvary). The seventh saying was profound because it reveals to us that Jesus had complete control over His faculties. For Him to make this statement during the horrible suffering He endured at the time of His death, He would have to remember, to the exact second, that the first Passover lamb was sacrificed in order to fulfill to the letter the prophetic type that the first lamb represented.

How could anyone know and have control over a situation like this? He would have to be God Himself to have in His mind the complete prophetic facts concerning the crucifixion. David prophesied in Psalm 31 the exact phrase Jesus would say at that moment. This was the seventh and final utterance made by Jesus before He died.

Psalm 31:5. *Into thine hand I commit my spirit: thou hast redeemed me, O LORD God of truth.*

Luke 23:46. *And when Jesus had cried with a loud voice, he said, Father, into thy hands I commend [commit] my spirit: and having said thus, he gave up the ghost.*

According to the Hebrew text of Psalm 31:6, starting with the second letter in the first word, counting forward every tenth letter spells *my Messiah; Mashiachi;* משיחי. The adjacent letters at the same ELS spell *the Lamb; Haseh;* השה.

I believe we can say with John the Baptist, *"Behold the Lamb of God, which taketh away the sin of the world"* (John 1:29).

Does God have a Son? This has been the debate among scholars and laymen since the first century. We know that God is one according the Shma in Deuteronomy 6. However, the book of Wisdom, Proverbs, gives us the answer to the argument.

Proverbs 30:4-5. (4) *Who has gone up to heaven, and come down? Who has gathered the wind in His fists? Who has bound the waters in His garments? Who has made all the ends of the earth to rise? What is His name, and what is His Son's name? Surely you know. (5) Every word of God is pure: He is a shield to those who seek refuge in Him.* [Interlinear Hebrew Bible]

Proverbs 30:4. Starting with the second letter in the 13th word, counting forward every 22nd letter spells *Jesus the Gift; Yeshua Shai;* שׁ ישוע.

John 3:16-17. (16) *For God so loved the world, that he gave his only begotten Son, that whosoever believeth in him should not perish but have everlasting life. (17) For God sent not his Son into the world to condemn the world; but that the world through him might be saved.*

Five

THE CROWNING PROPHECIES OF THE BIBLE

One of the most dynamic and significant of all the prophetic Scriptures referring to the coming Messiah, His life, and the price He would pay for our redemption is found in Isaiah 53. This chapter has been referred to as the *Suffering Servant* chapter, because it contains graphic details about the events leading up to the cross, the crucifixion, and the eternal benefits for all mankind. There is enough information on the surface reading that should convince anyone that our salvation hinges upon the fulfillment of this chapter.

For many years, some rabbis taught that these Scriptures were speaking of Israel the nation, not Jesus the Messiah. As a matter of fact, many Orthodox rabbis *deliberately* do *not* teach from these passages because of the ramifications of their explaining that these Scriptures obviously speak of a Man who would give His life as a ransom for many. *There is no possible way this chapter could refer to a nation, because the persecution of any nation does not have the power in that persecution to eradicate sins or save anyone.* This chapter *definitely* is referring to a specific Man.

The complete prophecy of Isaiah 53 starts in chapter 52:13. Within these prophetic verses are 801 letters, all uniquely designed and precisely written to convey the clearest picture of the coming Messiah who paid the price of redemption. There are at least fifty-seven prophecies in the Suffering Messiah passages. Jesus fulfilled each and every one of these, even to the smallest detail. *If He had been just a man,* with all the shortcomings of a human being, *He never would have had any control over the fulfillment of these prophecies.*

There are 16,931 words and 66,890 letters comprising the whole book of Isaiah. When the prophet wrote the book, he had been receiving glorious revelations from the Lord Himself. These revelations were for the benefit of all mankind. Around 745 B.C., Isaiah wrote:

In the year that king Uzziah died I saw also the Lord sitting upon a throne, high and lifted up, and his train filled the temple (Isaiah 6:1).

This was a heavenly vision of the Lord in the Temple of His glorious throne room. After Isaiah realized that he was not prepared for his calling, the Lord sent an angel, who touched the prophet's lips with a fiery coal from the altar in heaven. This gave the prophet a mouth that would speak, as it were, with tongues of fire. As a result of this experience, the prophet became a great orator and was inspired to write the magnificent book of Isaiah, which is mostly prophetic. It was not until after Isaiah's revelation of the Lord that he *knew* that he was being prepared for the heavenly calling that was set before him.

According to *Halley's Bible Handbook*, Isaiah "is quoted in the New Testament more than any other prophet. What a mind he had! In some of his rhapsodies he reaches heights unequaled even by Shakespeare, Milton, or Homer.... His martyrdom: A tradition, in the Talmud, which was accepted as authentic by the early Church Fathers, states that Isaiah resisted Manasseh's idolatrous decrees, and was fastened between two planks, and 'sawn asunder,' thus suffering a most horrible death. This is thought to be referred to in Hebrews 11:37." It is so amazing that Isaiah, the prophet who wrote of the crucifixion, suffered a similar death on a wooden cross.

The book of Isaiah is the crown jewel of all the books of the Old Testament. Of all the sixty-six chapters in this book, the 53rd chapter is considered by many Bible scholars to be the brightest sparkle of the jewel. It describes in vivid detail the Messiah's childhood, ministry, sacrificial death, and resurrection.

The 53rd chapter gives additional prophetic information with reference to the first Messianic prophecy in Genesis 3:15, which is a picture of the redemption of all mankind. It goes into the "fine print" description of the manner by which it would be fulfilled. This is one of the most beloved Scriptures in all the Bible. It describes the Servant of the Lord in His sufferings, and at times it seems as though Isaiah is speaking of the past tense.

His description of the prophecies are so vivid that you would think that Isaiah was standing at the foot of the cross of Calvary, but he wrote it many centuries *before* it was fulfilled by Jesus the Messiah.

Isaiah 52:13-15. (13) *Behold, my servant shall deal prudently, he shall be exalted and extolled, and be very high.* (14) *As many were astonished at thee; his visage was so marred more than any man, and his form more than the sons of men:* (15) *So shall he sprinkle many nations; the kings shall shut their mouths at him: for that which had not been told them shall they see; and that which they had not heard shall they consider.*

13 הנה ישכיל עבדי ירום ונשא וגבה מאד: כאשר שממו עליך

14 רבים כן־משחת מאיש מראהו ותארו מבני אדם: כן יזה

15 גוים רבים עליו יקפצו מלכים פיהם כי אשר

אל־ספר להם ראו ואשר לא־שמעו התבוננו:

There are at least seven prophecies within this text. In addition, there are encoded insights that reflect the surface reading of these prophecies.

Isaiah 52:13. Starting with the third letter in the second word, counting forward every seventh letter spells *for man (mankind); ki'adahm;* כי אדם.

Isaiah 52:14. Starting with the first letter in the fourth word, counting forward every 21st letter spells *vision of salvation; ro'ai Yaishah;* ראי ישעה.

Indeed, as the prophet Isaiah was writing this portion of Scripture, the Holy Spirit opened his understanding to some truly awesome insights. I believe what Isaiah saw in advance by the Spirit of God was the complete salvation of all mankind. I also believe that he received a profound revelation of the name of the Savior.

Isaiah 52:13. Starting with the first letter in the second word, counting forward and taking the first letter of every *seventh* word spells *Jesus appointed (designated); Yeshua sahman;* ישוע סמן.

The Holy Scriptures have identified the Servant of the Lord about whom Isaiah was writing. There is a scripture in the New Testament that comes to my mind at this point, and it tells us that Jesus was appointed to bring salvation through His suffering. *Now is my soul troubled; and what shall I say? Father, save me from this hour: but for this cause came I unto this hour* (John 12:27).

Jesus knew very well what His mission would be from the beginning, and He also knew that He would complete that responsibility on that foreordained day. There was absolutely no question in His mind that He would finish the heavenly charge, though He encountered temptations that anyone of us would have (Hebrews 4:15). Since He was God manifested in the flesh, He knew there would be hostile circumstances; nevertheless, He persevered through it all. He also knew that if He had not been sent from God, He would have faltered at the great commission.

The following verses from Isaiah tell us that Jesus was born as any child would be, but the great difference about Jesus was that His heavenly Father, through the Holy Spirit, conceived the holy child within the womb of Mary, His earthly mother. The phrase, *the Arm of the Lord*, is a term referring to the Messiah, who would grow up as any newborn baby would. Nevertheless, He had the highest calling of all. He was the Lamb of God and Savior of the world.

Isaiah 53:1-2. (1) *Who hath believed our report? and to whom is the arm of the LORD revealed? (2) For he shall grow up before him as a tender plant, and as a root out of a dry ground: he hath no form nor comeliness; and when we shall see him, there is no beauty that we should desire him.*

The reply to these two questions have a generation-to-generation answer. In the first generation (century), many believed God; thus, the Lord was revealed to them. And so it is today...to as many to believe the inspired reports about Him will He reveal Himself. Jesus came the first time when there had been no vision nor prophet for at least four centuries. The whole world was void, and there was a great famine in the land. The Good News and the Spirit of God had not moved in a mighty way for hundreds of years. The world was as though it was dry ground and without fertilization.

Jesus did not arrive on earth in His majestic splendor, nor did He appear with His heavenly grandeur. But He came as a baby and grew into manhood just as any other child would, but with an enduring innocence and without sin. The reason why He came in humility was to win the humble as well as the aristocratic. Had He come to us with regal fanfare and majestic splendor, the uniqueness of the mustard seed of faith could not have been tried as gold. Instead, many would have desired Him for His royalty and beauty. For to know Him is to love Him, and to believe Him is to receive Him in His horrendous and agonizing condition that was caused by our decrepit sin. So, by faith then, we shall behold Him in His majesty and heavenly Splendor, until that day when we shall see Him face to face.

Isaiah the prophet gives us a panoramic preview concerning His mission in this life and His destiny for the ages to come.

Isaiah 7:14-15. (14) *Therefore the Lord himself shall give you a sign; Behold, a virgin shall conceive, and bear a son, and shall call his name Immanuel.* (15) *Butter and honey shall he eat, that he may know to refuse the evil, and choose the good.*

Isaiah 7:15. Starting with the third letter in the sixth word, counting forward every 30th letter spells *Jesus; Yeshua;* ישוע.

Isaiah 7:19. Starting with the sixth letter in the seventh word, counting in reverse every 66th letter spells *Messiah; Mashiach;* משיח. The following letters at the same ELS spell *for the Lamb of God; kiseh El;* כסה־אל. Also, at the same ELS we find the *Lamb of the Lord; seh le'Adonai;* שה לאדני.

Could God have made anything clearer than these insights, identifying Jesus the Messiah as the Son whom the virgin would conceive? Also, that He would be the Lamb of God, and that His name would be called Immanuel?

Matthew 1:20-23. (20) *But while he thought on these things, behold, the angel of the Lord appeared unto him in a dream, saying,*

Joseph, thou son of David, fear not to take unto thee Mary thy wife: for that which is conceived in her is of the Holy Ghost. (21) And she shall bring forth a son, and thou shalt call his name JESUS: for he shall save his people from their sins. (22) Now all this was done, that it might be fulfilled which was spoken of the Lord by the prophet [Isaiah], saying, (23) Behold, a virgin shall be with child, and shall bring forth a son, and they shall call his name Immanuel, which being interpreted is, God with us.

Isaiah 9:6-7. (6) *For unto us a child [a tender plant] is born, unto us a son is given: and the government shall be upon his shoulder: and his name shall be called Wonderful, Counselor, The mighty God, The everlasting Father, The Prince of Peace. (7) Of the increase of his government and peace there shall be no end, upon the throne of David, and upon his kingdom, to order it, and to establish it with judgment and with justice from henceforth even for ever. The zeal of the Lord of hosts will perform this.*

The prophet is telling us that this child is God Himself who will take upon Himself the form of a baby and son. Additionally, these prophecies project us into the future, when the Messianic kingdom is set up by the Messiah, whose government will have no end, but will perpetually increase as time progresses.

1. A child is born.

2. A Son is given.

3. Government will be His responsibility.

4. His name, Wonderful.

5. His name, Counselor.

6. His name, The mighty God.

7. His name, The everlasting Father.

8. His name, The Prince of Peace.

I had always wondered whether or not the earthly name of the Person about whom the prophet was writing is encoded. Several years ago, while studying the Hebrew text in Isaiah 9, I was impressed by the Holy Spirit to search for His name in the codes. It was amazing what the Lord revealed to me from His Word.

Isaiah 9:5. From the Hebrew text, starting with the first letter in the 19th word, counting in reverse every 75th letter spells *Jesus; Yeshua;* ישוע.

The rejection of Jesus the Messiah came to pass exactly as the prophet had written. *He is despised and rejected of men; a man of sorrows, and acquainted with grief: and we hid as it were our faces from him; he was despised, and we esteemed him not* (Isaiah 53:3).

For instance, the disciple Peter was forewarned by the Lord that he would reject (deny) Him three times before the dawn of the day.

Peter answered and said unto him, Though all men shall be offended because of thee, yet will I never be offended. Jesus said unto him, Verily I say unto thee, That this night, before the cock crow, thou shalt deny me thrice (Matthew 26:33-34).

Not only did Peter deny Jesus three times, but he lied to others who confronted him about his denial. But when Peter looked into the eyes of his loving Savior and saw the innocence of this guiltless Lamb, it was as though Jesus was saying to him, "I knew you would deny Me, but I love you and I forgive you." It is so amazing about the love of God! He, through His Holy Spirit, allowed Peter to preach the very first sermon on the day of Pentecost ten days after His ascension.

Jesus was despised by the religious hierarchy of His day. The ecclesiastical arrangement that the Sanhedrim, Pharisees, and the Scribes had with the Roman rulers was convenient for their political and religious control over the people. Therefore, they rejected Jesus and His followers. Probably the strongest and most crucial rejection Jesus suffered was when the Romans, under pressure from the high priest and Sanhedrin, released a known murderer, whose name was Barabbas, instead of him.

This would be the second-to-the-last personal rejection that Jesus would suffer before He Himself was to be executed. The last rejection came while He and the two malefactors were enduring such horrific suffering, while nailed to their assigned crosses. One received Him as his personal Savior, but the other rejected Him. Today, as it has been revealed throughout history, *many* men, women, boys, and girls in every walk of life are reject-ing Him; by contrast, many others have believed the Holy Scriptures' inspired report of Him and are following Him. One day, all of us who have believed the report of the Good News, will follow Him into eternity, where we shall dwell in His presence for never-ending ages to come.

John 12:48. *He that rejecteth me, and receiveth not my words, hath one that judgeth him: the word that I have spoken, the same shall judge him in the last day.*

The verse in Isaiah 53:3 goes on to say that Jesus was *a man of sorrows, and acquainted with grief.*

Jesus was grieved and filled with great sorrow as He wept over Jerusalem because of their rejection of Him, and that this great city would be destroyed by the very ones who catered to the wishes of the Scribes, Pharisees, and Sanhedrin of that day. The prophecy is four-fold.

1. He *grieved* over His people who rejected Him.

2. He *took our grief* when He died upon the cross.

3. He *had great sorrow* for those who despised Him.

4. He *took our sorrow* when He died upon the cross.

We hid as it were our faces from him (Isaiah 53:3). This is an unusual statement. Perhaps it is best explained this way: At Golgotha, on that confusing and frightening day, while many of the people were milling about, gawking at Him, laughing at Him, taunting Him, screeching at Him, as He was absorbing within Himself the deepening impact of excruciating agonies and sorrows for all mankind's sins, *we* might just as well have been right there with them. In type and shadow we *were* and *are* there.

So, in effect, throughout these centuries we have also been looking upon Him who was beaten and tortured beyond recognition. Even though He was becoming a bloody pulp of flesh, the Holy Spirit of God within Him prevailed; the Son of God had no malice within Him. As we were looking into the face of this blood-spattered, dying Man, we began to (and do) realize that He took our place for our crimes against God. Yes, we saw then (and now we *do* see) our faces in Him on that day of unspeakable degradation.

It has even been said by the best Bible scholars that God the Father hid His face from Him on the darkest day in all of earth's history, when He took our vile sins. Our sins were so horrible that God Himself hid His face, as it were, from our transgressions. Beyond the shadow of a doubt, the appalling blasphemies of all mankind from every generation—past, present, and future—were laid upon the Lamb of God on that infamous, yet glorious, day, 2,000 years ago.

Isaiah 53:5. *But he was wounded for our transgressions, he was bruised for our iniquities: the chastisement of our peace was upon him; and with his stripes we are healed.*

There are four major thoughts in this verse that explain, in measure, why Jesus was so hideously tortured and mutilated during those twelve long, grueling hours before He died upon the cross.

1. *Wounded for our transgressions.* On the 14th day of Aviv, at about three o'clock in the morning, Jesus was incarcerated. He was spit upon, slapped, ridiculed, and degraded many times more than any other person could be.

2. *He was bruised for our iniquities.* He was hit repeatedly about His body as He was led from one court session to another.

3. *He was chastised (received punishment) for our peace.* The records of the New Testament tell us that Jesus was constantly mocked and harassed by the Jewish leaders and the mobs. The Romans also contributed their share to this degrading performance against Jesus.

4. *With His stripes we are healed.* He received at least thirty-nine lashes from the Roman whip. Attached to each strand of the whip were at least nine strips with bone, metal hooks, and stone. This was sometimes called the cat-of-nine tails, which would make 351 gashes in His face, back, and chest. Each time this whip was retrieved for an additional strike, it would tear loose His flesh from His body. This was the usual Roman method of punishing people before they were to be executed upon the cross.

In light of the gory scenes described above, one might wonder how many people survived to even be nailed to their personal crosses. However, there were many times, according to Roman history, when they were lenient with this type of whipping, but not so in the case of Jesus.

As you reflect upon this scene, you will see that Jesus took upon Himself every sin and sickness since the beginning of time. Can you add them up? Is it perhaps 10,000 for each person, or could there be many more? Only God knows. From our carnal minds of limited reasoning, there are just too many sins to calculate, but God knew what it would take to justify every person since the time of Adam and Eve.

There are some encoded prophetic phrases in a section of the Scripture relating to the events of that day.

Isaiah 53:5. Starting with the second letter in the sixth word, counting forward every 21st letter spells *pierced in His flesh; chollah basaro;* מחללה בשרו.

Jesus was pierced by the stripes He received, the crown of thorns that was placed on His head, and by the nails that were driven into His feet and hands. Then the Roman soldier pierced His side with a spear, and from that wound flowed blood and water (John 19:34).

Isaiah 53:3. Starting with the third letter in the eighth word, counting in reverse every 18th letter spells *water; blood; mayim; dahm;* מים־דם.

John 20:27. *Then saith he to Thomas, Reach hither thy finger, and behold my hands; and reach hither thy hand, and thrust it into my side: and be not faithless, but believing.*

There is a stunning array of encoded insights within Isaiah 53, giving us additional information that is verified in the New Testament, where Jesus fulfilled these prophecies.

Isaiah 53:6-12. *(6) All we like sheep have gone astray; we have turned every one to his own way; and the LORD hath laid on him [Jesus] the iniquity of us all. (7) He was oppressed, and he was afflicted, yet he opened not his mouth: he is brought as a lamb to the slaughter, and as a sheep before her shearers is dumb, so he openeth not his mouth. (8) He was taken from prison and from judgment: and who shall declare his generation? for he was cut off out of the* *land of the living: for the transgression of my people was he stricken. (9)And he made his grave with the wicked, and with the rich in his death; because he had done no violence, neither was any deceit in his mouth. (10) Yet it pleased the LORD to bruise him; he hath put him to grief: when thou shalt make his soul an offering for sin, he shall see his seed, he shall prolong his days, and the pleasure of the LORD shall prosper in his hand. (11) He shall see of the travail of his soul, and shall be satisfied: by his knowledge shall my righteous servant justify many; for he shall bear their iniquities. (12) Therefore will I divide him a portion with the great, and he shall divide the spoil with the strong; because he hath poured out his soul unto death: and he was numbered with the transgressors; and he bare the sin of many, and made intercession for the transgressors.*

Isaiah 53:10. Starting with the fourth letter in the 11th word, counting in reverse every 20th letter spells *Jesus is my name; Yeshua shmi;* ישוע שמי.

This encoded insight again reveals to us the name of the Person about whom the prophet was writing. Please notice that the encoded statement that was just mentioned was written from the position of the first person, and He was speaking of Himself. This gives us full comprehension of the magnitude of this insight.

This very special insight, which was placed there by God's Holy Spirit, should settle for all time the controversy that has persisted for many centuries about the name of the Person to whom Isaiah was referring in chapter 53. If your heart is beginning to open up to thoughts pertaining to matters of the Spirit of

God, I trust that this same insight will help to settle this controversy for *you*, once and for all.

About eight years ago, as I began to discover the full and vivid complexities of insights in this matrix at 20-ELS, I was completely overwhelmed—and feeling so insignificant—at the unfolding and massive dimensions of the Word of God. It was continually revealing the authenticity and the character of the Person about whom the prophet was writing.

Isaiah 53:11. Starting with the fifth letter in the ninth word, counting in reverse every 20th letter spells מעל ישוע שמי עז. This complete sentence from the Hebrew transliterates and translates, respectively: *ma'al Yeshua shmi ahz; from above (highly exalted), Jesus is my strong name.* At the same ELS the adjacent letters spell *the Lamp (light) of Jehovah; nair Adonai;* נר יהוה.

The six Hebrew words, according to the Hebrew insight revealed to us in this series of codes, are more clearly explained from the point of view of the New Testament.

1. *From above.*

John 8:23. *And he [Jesus] said unto them, Ye are from beneath; I am from above: ye are of this world; I am not of this world.*

2. *Jesus is my strong name.*

Matthew 28:18. *And Jesus came and spake unto them, saying, All power is given unto me in heaven and in earth.*

Philippians 2:9-11. (9) *Wherefore God also hath highly exalted him, and given him a name which is above every name:*

(10) *That at the name of Jesus every knee should bow, of things in heaven, and things in earth, and things under the earth.* (11) *And that every tongue should confess that Jesus Christ is Lord, to the glory of God the Father.*

3. *Lamp of the Lord.*

John 8:12. *Then spake Jesus again unto them, saying, I am the light of the world: he that followeth me shall not walk in darkness, but shall have the light of life.*

A mathematical analysis was performed on the phrase, *from above, Jesus is my strong name.* The result? It was out of the range of accidental occurrences. The odds were .000000 to one million that this statement could happen by chance. Another analysis calculated the odds as being from one to 50 quadrillion that it could happen by chance. Here again, the ineffable Word of God gives us proof that it originated from beyond earth's space and time dimensions. Only God could have embedded these codes for us to find, therefore, enabling us to validate His Word and that we may give *Him* all the glory.

In the ninth chapter of Daniel, the prophet gives us several prophecies concerning the coming Messiah who would be cut off in death, but not for Himself. For many years some rabbis taught that the Messiah who would be cut off in death was Hezekiah, or someone like him. But the Scripture reveals the name of the Messiah who would give His life for someone else...each of us.

Daniel 9:26. *And after threescore and two weeks shall Messiah be cut off, but not for himself.*

Daniel 9:26. Starting with the fourth letter in the ninth word, counting in reverse every 26th letter spells *Jesus; Yeshua;* ישוע. The adjacent letters at the same ELS spell *Jehovah; Adonai;* יהוה. What a wonderful discovery this is—*to know for sure* that the person about whom Daniel was speaking was not one of the prophets of old, but the Lord Jesus Himself.

If these were the only insights encoded within the Hebrew Masoretic Text, it would be enough proof for any open-minded person. But there is more—much more—to learn from the hidden messages, giving credence to the magnificent written Word.

There were three women and one man around the cross when Jesus was crucified, not including the four Roman soldiers. These four people were very close to Him, even during His most desperate hours. Though everyone else had deserted Him, these few were the dedicated loved ones who stayed close to Him while the most hideous blasphemies were being performed against Him.

The disciple John was one of them, but later he, like the others, ran and hid himself from the angry mobs who had slandered Jesus and His teachings. During the grueling hours leading up to the time of the death of Jesus on His cross, the anticipation of His calling upon legions of angels was intensely felt by all who had followed Him prior to His arrest. When He did not call for assistance, they were painfully disappointed, and great fear overtook most of them. Apparently, they forgot about all the prophesies describing His death.

The names of the four people who were around the cross of

Jesus are encoded in the same verse where the above code, *my name is Jesus*, is found. Of all the disciples, John was considered to be the closest to Jesus during His earthly ministry. It seemed as though John was always with Him, except on a few occasions when Jesus needed to be alone. In light of the previous statement, it is so interesting that the first letter in the apostle John's name is encoded with the same first letter where I found the name of Jesus.

Isaiah 53:10. Starting with the fourth letter in the 11th word, counting in reverse every 28th letter spells *John; Yochanan;* יוחנן.

The names of the three women, all of whom were named Mary and accompanied John to the cross when Jesus was being crucified, are also encoded in the very same area of Scripture. It seems as though they were predestined to be the closest to Jesus, until after His death. Salome, the wife of Zebedee, is jointly encoded with the others. Below are the details of their ELS codes.

Mary +6. Mary -23. Mary -44. Salome -15. John -28.

John 19:25-26. *(25) Now there stood by the cross of Jesus his mother [Mary], and his mother's sister [Salome], Mary the wife of Cleophas, and Mary Magdalene. (26) When Jesus therefore saw his mother, and the disciple [John] standing by, whom he loved, he saith unto his mother, Woman, behold thy son!*

Mark 15:40. *There were also women looking on afar off: among whom was Mary Magdalene, and Mary the mother of James the less and of Joses, and Salome.*

In Isaiah 53, there are hundreds of names of people, places, and events encoded that are directly associated with Jesus on the days preceding His arrest, trials, and crucifixion. Without going into too much detail at this time, I will only show seventy-four of the names, places, and events of that time period.

---

1. Jesus
2. Nazarene
3. Messiah
4. Shiloh
5. Passover
6. Galilee
7. Herod
8. Caesar
9. The evil Roman city
10. Caiaphas
11. Annas
12. Mary
13. Mary
14. Mary
15. Salome
16. The disciples
17. Peter
18. Matthew
19. John
20. Andrew
21. Thomas
22. Philip
23. James
24. James
25. Simon
26. Thaddaeus
27. Matthias
28. Let Him be crucified
29. His cross
30. Lamp of the Lord
31. His signature
32. Bread
33. Wine
34. From Zion
35. Moriah
36. Vinegar
37. Gall
38. Servant
39. David
40. Jesse
41. Blood
42. Water
43. From the atonement Lamb
44. The Seed
45. Levites
46. Joseph
47. Mary weeps
48. Moses
49. Elijah
50. The Prophet
51. Priest
52. The King
53. Praise Him
54. God
55. Tabernacle
56. Temple
57. Serpent
58. Daniel
59. Day of my glory
60. Shechem
61. Three crosses
62. The Lion
63. The Lamb
64. Peace
65. Aviv (month of Passover)
66. The oak tree
67. Perfection
68. Power
69. Strength
70. Savior
71. Goat
72. My Spirit
73. The ram
74. The whip

The sixth statement Jesus made before He entrusted the return of His Spirit to the Father was: *"It is finished!"* That statement was the official heavenly announcement, *legally and permanently* bringing into blood-purchased fulfillment the Lamb of God's promised redemption of all past, present, and future generations. That powerful statement carries us all the way back to the Garden of Eden where Adam and Eve *willingly* disobeyed their Creator. As a result of Adam and Eve's sins, all of mankind from that time forward was burdened with the death penalty of sin. "It is finished!" states beyond a shadow of a doubt that we have been *redeemed* from the *curse of the law*! From that moment to this— and for untold ages to come—it reverberates....

Isaiah 53:7. Starting with the second letter in the 13th word, counting forward every 30th letter spells *Adam;* אדם. Adjacent letters, also at 30-ELS, spell *Eve,* חוה; *man,* איש; and *woman,* אשה. To reiterate the theme in the preceding paragraph, this signifies that Jesus paid the price for redemption for *Adam* and *Eve* as well as for every *man* and *woman* who has ever been born into this world since the beginning of time and for the ages to come. Our Savior completed our redemption, but it will not benefit you or me unless we call upon Him for everlasting salvation.

The evidence thus far is monumental and breathtaking, and it is continually revealing to all of us the importance of the sacrifice made by Jesus our Messiah for the whole world. For God to have placed all this information on the surface reading, interwoven with the encoded words, phrases, and sentences, again

proves that He has a holy desire that all people—including you—
come to Him with sincere and open hearts to receive the Lamb
of God as their—and your—Substitute for their sins and for the
salvation of their—and your—soul. He died for *you!*

Six

THE RETURN
OF THE MESSIAH

After Jesus rose victoriously from the grave, He continued to teach many deep spiritual matters. He gave additional instructions to His followers and told them to stay in Jerusalem until they were endued with the mighty power from on high. It was not until forty days later that He ascended into heaven and sat down on the right hand of the Majesty on high. There were at least five hundred men and women present when Jesus was caught up into a cloud and entered heaven on our behalf. He now sits on the right hand of God as our High Priest to make intercession for us according to the loving graciousness of His everlasting divine character.

PROCLAIMING THE GOSPEL WITH POWER

Matthew 28:18. *And Jesus came and spake unto them, saying, all power is given unto me in heaven and in earth.*

Luke 24:49. *And, behold, I send the promise of my Father upon you: but tarry ye in the city of Jerusalem, until ye be endued with power from on high.*

Acts 1:4-11. (4) *And, being assembled together with them, commanded them that they should not depart from Jerusalem, but wait for the promise of the Father, which, saith he, ye have heard of me.* (5) *For John truly baptized with water; but ye shall be baptized with the Holy Ghost not many days hence.* (6) *When they therefore were come together, they asked of him, saying, Lord, wilt thou at this time restore again the kingdom to Israel?* (7) *And he said unto them, It is not for you to know the times or the seasons, which the Father hath put in his own power.* (8) *But ye shall receive power, after that the Holy Ghost is come upon you: and ye shall be witnesses unto me both in Jerusalem, and in all Judea, and in Samaria, and unto the uttermost part of the earth.* (9) *And when he had spoken these things, while they beheld, he was taken up; and a cloud received him out of their sight.* (10) *And while they looked steadfastly toward heaven as he went up, behold, two men stood by them in white apparel;* (11) *Which also said, Ye men of Galilee, why stand ye gazing up into heaven? this same Jesus, which is taken up from you into heaven, shall so come in like manner as ye have seen him go into heaven.*

There are seven points from the Scriptures that I want to note.

1. Jesus received all power in heaven and on earth.

2. The disciples were not to be concerned with the times and seasons of the political reestablishment of Israel and the Messianic kingdom.

3. They were to tarry in Jerusalem until they were endued with power from on high.

4. They shall be baptized with the Holy Spirit and with power.

5. They shall be Jesus' witnesses in all the world, beginning in Jerusalem.

6. Jesus ascended into heaven.

7. Jesus, in the same manner as He departed earth, will return to the same place from which He departed—the Mount of Olives.

After Jesus ascended into heaven, He sent the Holy Spirit to those who were waiting for the promise of the Father. There were one hundred and twenty of His original five hundred followers who continued in the commandment to wait for that promise (Acts 1:15). It was not until ten days later (fifty days after His resurrection) that the Feast of *Shavuot*, שבועת; *Pentecost* was gloriously fulfilled. The same experience of Pentecost is being fulfilled in the lives of millions of people today through the baptism of the Holy Spirit with fire. It is through this supernatural method that He forms and transforms His Body of true believers.

Acts 2:1-4. (1) *And when the day of Pentecost [Shavuot] was fully come, they were all with one accord in one place. (2) And suddenly there came a sound from heaven as of a rushing mighty wind, and it filled all the house where they were sitting. (3) And there appeared unto them cloven tongues like as of fire, and it sat upon each of them. (4) And they were all filled with the Holy Ghost, and began to speak with other tongues, as the Spirit gave them utterance.*

When Jesus was teaching in the Temple, He revealed that He was the living water; and that if any man was thirsty for this water of life, he was to come to Him (John 7:37-39). Jesus would give them water flowing as the Holy Spirit-anointed rivers of salvation. This wonderful truth has been experienced in type and shadow by the children of Israel throughout their history.

When Israel came out of their bondage in Egypt, they began to wander in the desert. Because of His infinite mercy and grace, God led them to a place with twelve wells of water and seventy palm trees. This oasis—a comfort station in a dry place—supplied them with life-giving sustenance for their journey that lay just ahead. Though it was an *immediate* blessing to them, this experience had a *futuristic* fulfillment as well.

Exodus 15:27. *And they came to Elim, where were twelve wells of water, and threescore and ten palm trees: and they encamped there by the waters.*

Exodus 15:27. Starting with the third letter in the 13th word, which is *the waters;* המים, counting forward every 235th letter spells *the Lord Jesus; Adonai Yeshua;* יהוה ישוע.

Exodus 15:26. Starting with the first letter in the 17th word, counting forward every ninth letter spells *the King of my salvation; ha'melek hoshai'ai;* המלך הושיעי.

The Lord Jesus is our source of *all* life-giving water, which represents *the living water* that flows from the throne of God in heaven. We are *commanded* of the Lord to be filled with His spiritual water, which is *the baptism of the Holy Spirit.*

John 7:37-39. (37) *In the last day, that great day of the feast, Jesus stood and cried, saying, If any man thirst, let him come unto me, and drink.* (38) *He that believeth on me, as the scripture hath said, out of his belly shall flow rivers of living water.* (39) *(But this spake he of the Spirit, which they that believe on him should receive: for the Holy Ghost was not yet given; because that Jesus was not yet glorified.)*

During the Feast of Tabernacles, Jesus was in the Temple, where He quoted from Isaiah 12.

Isaiah 12:2-4. (2) *Behold, God is my salvation; I will trust, and not be afraid: for the Lord JEHOVAH is my strength and my song; he also is become my salvation [Yeshua].* (3) *Therefore with joy shall ye draw water out of the wells of salvation [Yeshua].* (4) *And in that day shall ye say, Praise the LORD, call upon his name, declare his doings among the people, make mention that his name is exalted.*

These Scriptures have had a partial fulfillment since Jesus quoted them in the Temple. From that time onward to this present age, many people have experienced the wells of living water flowing as gushing torrents, bringing deliverance and salvation to all people who will call upon Jesus. The ultimate fulfillment of this prophecy will be realized during the Seventh Day—the millennium.

Since the time of the first outpouring of the Spirit of God on the day of Pentecost, the Lord has been calling millions of witnesses, ministers, missionaries, and teachers to proclaim the Good News around the world. However, until this present generation, it was not possible to preach the Gospel to every nation simultaneously. Aided by a wide variety of twenty-first-century telecommunications—especially by satellite and Internet—plus rapidly increasing global air travel, I believe that all the vivid prophecies of Daniel, as well as the Bible's other prophecies of end-time events, are being fulfilled at an exponential rate.

Daniel 12:4. *But thou, O Daniel, shut up the words, and seal the book, even to the time of the end: many shall run to and fro, and knowledge shall be increased.*

Matthew 24:14. *And this gospel of the kingdom shall be preached in all the world for a witness unto all nations; and then shall the end come.*

This is the answer to the disciples' question in Acts 1:6: *Lord, wilt thou at this time restore again the kingdom?* Jesus responded, *It is not for you to know the times or the seasons.* Jesus was telling them not to be concerned with the end-time events, as we understand them to be. He reminded His disciples that they *must fulfill* the Great Commission in their era as His witnesses. *They must declare the Good News!*

However, God has ordained believers in this generation to fulfill the Final Commission, and at the same time He wants us to watch for the signs of the end of this age and to be prepared *for His soon return to earth.* Certainly, we can better understand that the information that describes the last generation before Jesus returns also paints a vivid and prophetic picture of a time of explosive increases of knowledge in every field of communication and transportation.

This has a two-fold meaning. First, computer technology and software provide educational resources through the Internet, which enables people to "run to and fro" during these hectic times. Second, most of us can fly just about anywhere we can afford to go. These brilliantly designed inventions are the main "vehicles" helping to promote the Good News—the Gospel— during these last days.

Since the first century, God has given to every generation the same heavenly and holy calling on their lives: *Be My witnesses.* But the statement, *It is not for you to know the times or the seasons,* is being used today by some people who do not teach the Lord's imminent return to earth. They honestly believe it is not for us to know the times and the seasons for our day. However, I take exception to this thought, because the Bible plainly teaches us to be aware of the signs of the end of this age and to preach the blessed hope, the soon return of the Lord.

The phrase, *all power,* is powerful in itself. Consider for a moment all the power and capacity of heaven and earth. There is no greater dynamism than that of our Savior, who has destroyed the powers of darkness and shares His authority and power with anyone who will follow Him. This power and authority is ordained by God's Holy Spirit to help His true believers overcome all satanic deceptions of the carnal mind's reasoning and for witnessing in this day, precisely as it was at the beginning of the church age. We are called to minister to the spiritual and natural needs of all people everywhere, always proclaiming the power of the blood of Jesus and the testimony He has given.

We are the Temple of God because He dwells within us. As we proclaim the Good News, God will add to His Body as the Holy Spirit draws them. God places all of us in His Body as it pleases Him; we are the Body of Christ and a holy Temple who exalt and praise the Lord in all that we do in His name.

Ephesians 2:19-22. *(19) Now therefore ye are no more strangers and foreigners, but fellow citizens with the saints, and of the household of God; (20) And are built upon the foundation of the apostles and prophets, Jesus Christ himself being the chief corner stone; (21) In whom all the building fitly framed together groweth unto an holy temple in the Lord: (22) In whom ye also are builded together for a habitation of God through the Spirit.*

Zechariah 6:12-13. *(12) And speak unto him, saying, Thus speaketh the LORD of hosts, saying, Behold the man whose name is The BRANCH; and he shall grow up out of his place, and he shall build the temple of the LORD: (13) Even he shall build the temple of the LORD; and he shall bear the glory, and shall sit and rule upon his throne; and he shall be a priest upon his throne: and the counsel of peace shall be between them both.*

The Branch is a term used for the Messiah. These verses tell us that He, The Branch, shall be a Priest and a King, and He shall build the Temple of the Lord of hosts. The ultimate fulfillment of these Scriptures will be in the millennium.

Zechariah 6:15. *And they that are far off shall come and* *build in the temple of the LORD, and ye shall know that the LORD of hosts hath sent me unto you. And this shall come to pass, if ye will diligently obey the voice of the LORD your God.*

ורחוקים יבאו ובנו בהיכל יהוה וידעתם

כי־יהוה צבאות שלחני אליכם והיה

אם־שמוע תשמעון בקול יהוה אלהיכם:

Starting with the third letter in the 11th word, counting in reverse every seventh letter spells *Jesus; Yeshua;* ישוע.

The Hebrew words from which His encoded name are taken tell us that Jesus was sent by God to us and that we should know Him. However, to know Him personally would take a revelation by the Spirit of God.

1. *and you shall know;* וידעתם.

2. *Jehovah;* יהוה.

3. *has sent me;* שלחני.

4. *to you;* אליכם.

Though this Scripture is related to the millennium, it has an everyday fulfillment when we build up the Body of Christ, the holy Temple of the Lord.

It is *very* important to take notice of each word where a letter spelling out the encoded name of Jesus is located. I consider this combination of codes four-fold. The arrangement of this verse was orchestrated by a power outside our time-and-space dimensions. (1) Equidistant Letter Sequence. (2) This is related to the rebuilding of the Temple in the time of Zerubbabel, which was yet future when Zechariah wrote this. (3) It gives us an everyday commitment to add to and edify the Body of Christ in our generation. (4) Since this is Messianic in nature, it alludes to something else related to the subject matter, such as *the millennium Temple* where people from around the world will donate their efforts in building the Temple.

The ELS is the revelation of the name of *Jesus (Yeshua)* encoded. The directional codes are words and phrases referring to the complete restoration of the nation of Israel and the Temple. Furthermore, it refers to the Messianic projection of future events associated with the surface reading. In other words, it gives us references to different events that are related to one another.

THE RAPTURE AND RETURN OF CHRIST

The prophet Malachi paints for us a very clear picture of the rapture and return of the Lord Jesus with His saints.

Malachi 3:16-18. (16) *Then they that feared the LORD spake often one to another: and the LORD hearkened, and heard it, and a book of remembrance was written before him for them that feared the LORD, and that thought upon his name. (17) And they shall be mine, saith the LORD of hosts, in that day when I make up my jewels; and I will spare them, as a man spareth his own son that serveth him. (18) Then shall ye return, and discern between the righteous and the wicked, between him that serveth God and him that serveth him not.*

There are at least three major topics in these three verses, vital in the light they shed on the theme of the rapture and the second coming as two separate future events.

1. The Lord is aware of those who reverence Him, who talk about Him, and who meditate upon His name.

2. A book of remembrance is written before the Lord about the spiritual activity of His righteous saints.

3. He will gather His jewels (the righteous), then we shall return with Him to judge upon the earth.

In the day when the Lord calls us home, the books will be opened, and the judgment of the redeemed will take place. This judgment is for the rewarding of those people who are washed in the blood of the Lamb and have fulfilled their calling in this life. (Special note: The ancient Hebrew sages always taught that the book of remembrance, among others, will be opened on the day of the resurrection of the righteous dead.)

God gathers His precious jewels from this earth. This theme speaks of a process of refinement that takes place in bringing forth the purest of gems. When the jeweler finds a valuable stone that is in the rough, he patiently processes it by removing the flaws and dross that hinder the radiance of its beauty. When the Master Jeweler refines and completes *us* to perfection, we shall reflect the handiwork of the divine character of the Master Himself.

We are now perfect in His eyes, because He sees us as a finished and perfected product. From our natural perspective, we see the unfinished and imperfect portions of ourselves. The value of something is determined by the price that is paid for it. The price that was paid for *you and me* was all that heaven could afford—the life and death of the Son of God. No greater price than this could have been paid to purchase our salvation.

The ultimate theme of believers returning with the Lord to judge upon this earth is echoed throughout the Old and New Testaments. To return from a place, you must first arrive at the place from where you will be returning. Enoch's theme of the end-time describes the details: *And Enoch also, the seventh from Adam, prophesied of these, saying, Behold, the Lord cometh with ten thousands of his saints, to execute judgment upon all, and to convince all that are ungodly among them of all their ungodly deeds which they have ungodly committed, and of all their hard speeches which ungodly sinners have spoken against him* (Jude 14-15).

The Scripture teaches us not to judge anyone, but we can judge all things by the Spirit of God. It is not yet time for the final judgment of the wicked, but the time is coming in the very near future when all people will be judged according to the Word of God. The righteous are joint-heirs with the Lord Jesus, not only for the blessings of today, but in the consummation of all things. We shall rule and reign with Him throughout the ages to come!

The apostle Paul wrote a letter to the early church on the subject of *the rapture (caught up)*, which has a message for every generation of believers since the beginning of time.

1 Thessalonians 4:13-18. (13) *But I would not have you to be ignorant, brethren, concerning them which are asleep, that ye sorrow not, even as others which have no hope.* (14) *For if we* *believe that Jesus died and rose again, even so them also which sleep in Jesus will God bring with him. (15) For this we say unto you by the word of the Lord, that we which are alive and remain unto the coming of the Lord shall not prevent [precede] them which are asleep. (16) For the Lord himself shall descend from heaven with a shout, with the voice of the archangel, and with the trump of God: and the dead in Christ shall rise first: (17) Then we which are alive and remain shall be caught up together with them in the clouds, to meet the Lord in the air: and so shall we ever be with the Lord. (18) Wherefore comfort one another with these words.*

Paul described in detail the theme of the blessed hope of all believers, the rapture of the living and the dead. Oh what a glorious day that will be when Jesus comes and receives us unto Himself. The theme of glory will be on our lips: *Worthy is the Lamb that was slain to receive power, and riches, and wisdom, and strength, and honor, and glory, and blessing* (Revelation 5:12).

THE RAPTURE OF BELIEVERS
WITHIN A CERTAIN TIME PERIOD

There are several Scriptures I want to bring out at this time that give us a clearer understanding of what has been taking place between the first and second comings of the Lord Jesus Christ. The first coming deals with His birth, ministry, death, resurrection, and ascension. The second coming concerns His return to earth and the millennial reign of Christ on earth. However, prior to the second advent of Christ, the rapture must take place according to the Holy Scriptures.

THE RAPTURE CODE

Isaiah 9:2-3. (2) *The people who walk in darkness have seen a great light. The ones who dwell in the land of the shadow of death—Light has shone on them.* (3) *You have multiplied the nation; You have increased the joy. They rejoice before You as in the joy of harvest, as men shout when they divide the plunder.* [The Interlinear Bible]

The people that have walked in darkness have seen a great light. This statement refers to the light of the glorious Gospel of our Lord and Savior, Jesus the Messiah. Only those who accept the blood of atonement given freely by the Passover Lamb of God will receive the glorious light of their salvation. These are they who will be caught up to the throne of God in heaven when Jesus returns for His Body, the Church. This is called *the rapture.*

There are several encrypted Bible codes throughout these Scriptures that elucidate for us the biblical truth about the rapture and resurrection of all believers. This was explained by the apostle Paul in the New Testament.

Isaiah 9:2. Starting with the first letter in the seventh word, counting in reverse every 41st letter spells *enter into the rapture; bo ha'natzal;* בוא הנצל. Another way of saying this is to *go in the rapture.*

Isaiah 8:23. Starting with the third letter in the tenth word, counting in reverse every 39th letter spells *code; tzaphan;* צפן. The adjacent letters at the same ELS spell *the rapture;* נצל and *the blood;* הדם. It is because of the shed blood of Jesus that we have redemption. For without the shedding of blood there is no remission of sin.

Isaiah 9:2. Starting with the third letter in the tenth word, counting in reverse every 14th letter spells *the great harvest of Shiloh; Shiloh megal gadolah;* שׁילה מגל גדלה. Shiloh is a term for the Messiah as recorded in Genesis 49:10. *The sceptre shall not depart from Judah, nor a lawgiver from between his feet, until Shiloh come; and unto him shall the gathering of the people be.*

THE YESHUA CODES

When Moses brought forth the whole house of Israel from the Egyptian bondage, he was instructed by God to lead them to Mount Sinai in the desert of Arabia. On the fiftieth day from their departure from Egypt, the Lord told Moses to ascend to the mountaintop where He would meet with him. This meeting was on the fiftieth day after they crossed through the Red Sea and were freed from the bondage of their oppressors. This was the very first Feast of Pentecost (Shavuot) in the record of the Holy Bible. We can readily see a type of rapture when Moses ascended up to the mountain and God descended to meet him there.

Exodus 19 ties in with 1 Thessalonians 4:13-18 and John 14:1-3. When the Lord Himself shall descend from heaven, the believers, both alive and dead, shall ascend up to meet Him in the air.

John 14:1-3. (1) *Let not your heart be troubled: ye believe in God, believe also in me.* (2) *In my Father's house are many mansions:*

if it were not so, I would have told you. I go to prepare a place for you. (3) And if I go and prepare a place for you, I will come again, and receive you unto myself; that where I am, there ye may be also.

Exodus 19:16-20. *(16) And it came to pass on the third day in the morning, that there were thunders and lightnings, and a thick cloud upon the mount, and the voice of the trumpet exceeding loud; so that all the people that was in the camp trembled. (17) And Moses brought forth the people out of the camp to meet with God; and they stood at the nether part of the mount. (18) And mount Sinai was altogether on a smoke, because the LORD descended upon it in fire: and the smoke thereof ascended as the smoke of a furnace, and the whole mount quaked greatly. (19) And when the voice of the trumpet sounded long, and waxed louder and louder, Moses spake, and God answered him by a voice. (20) And the LORD came down upon mount Sinai, on the top of the mount: and the LORD called Moses up to the top of the mount; and Moses went up.*

Exodus 19:17. Starting with the fifth letter in the ninth word, counting forward every 26th letter spells *code; tzaphan;* צפן. The adjacent letters at 26-ELS spell *Jesus; Yeshua;* ישוע. Also, in this same sequence I found the Hebrew phrase, *my words are forever; dabari le' ha'olom;* דברי להעולם. In this same sequence *the Lamb; ha'seh;* השה is encoded.

1. My words are forever.
2. Jesus; Yeshua.
3. The Lamb.
4. Code.

This text also provides a very interesting combination that sheds additional light on the theme of the *rapture*. The biblical term for *rapture* is *natzal;* נצל. However, the *modern* Hebrew for rapture is *shilhuv;* שלהוב. Both of these combinations are encoded within the text.

Exodus 19:16. Starting with the fifth letter in the third word, counting in reverse every other letter spells *in (the) rapture;* שלהוב. To add additional proof of this event, the biblical word for *the rapture;* הנצל is encoded at a very low ELS at least four times throughout the text. The Hebrew word for *bride* is *kalah;* כלה, which accompanies each of these insights. Throughout the New Testament the Body of Christ is always referred to as the *Bride of Christ.*

The prophet Hosea sheds additional light on this precious subject and confirms the same insights, which refer directly to the *rapture.*

Hosea 6:1-3. (1) *Come, and let us return unto the LORD: for he hath torn, and he will heal us; he hath smitten, and he will bind us up. (2) After two days will he revive us: in the third day he will raise us up, and we shall live in his sight. (3) Then shall we know, if we follow on to know the LORD: his going forth is prepared as the morning; and he shall come unto us as the rain, as the latter and former rain unto the earth.*

1 לכו ונשובה אל־יהוה כי הוא טרף וירפאנו יך

ויחבשנו: 2 יחיינו מימים ביום השלישי יקמנו ונחיה

לפניו: 3 ונדעה נרדפה לדעת את־יהוה כשחר נכון

מצאו ויבוא כנשם לנו כמלקוש יורה ארץ:

It is believed by many Bible scholars that the third day mentioned by Hosea foreshadows the Messianic kingdom. The first two days refer to the time when Jesus (Yeshua) walked on earth two thousand years ago, and the third day alludes to the 1,000-year Messianic kingdom, when Jesus will reign on earth with the Church, His Body of born-again believers (2 Peter 3:8).

Hosea 6:2. *In the third day; bayom ha'shlishi;* ביום השלישי. Starting with the *shin* (שׁ) to the far left, taking every other letter from left to right spells *shilhuv;* שלהוב. This is a modern Hebrew word that means *the rapture.*

Starting with the *lamed* (ל) in the same phrase, *ha'shlishi;* השלישי, counting every 132nd letter from right to left spells *natzal;* נצל in reverse, which means *to be snatched up; rescued.* The adjacent letters at the same ELS spell *shachah;* שחה, which means *reverence; worship; praise.*

Hosea 6:6. Starting with the fourth letter, which is the *yod* (י) in the seventh word, which is *God;* אלהים, counting every 60th letter from right to left spells *Jesus; Yeshua;* ישוע. The adjacent letters at the same ELS spell *my Priest; Kohani;* כהני.

Hosea 6:10. Starting with the fourth letter in the sixth word, counting every fifth letter from left to right spells *the great month of Tishri; Tishrai rabah;* תשרי רבה. This month is when the last three Feasts of the Lord occur. They take place in the following order: 1. *(Jewish New Year) Rosh Hashanah, which is the Feast of Trumpets;* 2. *(Day of Atonement) Yom Kippur;* 3. *(Tabernacles) Sukkot.* The month of Tishrai generally comes in the month of September on the Gregorian calendar.

ESTHER, A PROPHETIC SYMBOL
OF THE PERFECTED BODY OF CHRIST

Esther had a mother's heart for her people, the Jews, who were held in captivity by the Persians. She laid her life on the line to bring deliverance to her kinsmen. In a time of trouble, she approached the king, who was also her husband, and presented her petition before the king on behalf of her countrymen. There is an awesome prophetic picture that unfolds in this great event.

Esther 5:1. *Now it came to pass on the third day, that Esther put on her royal apparel, and stood in the inner court of the king's house, over against the king's house: and the king upon his royal throne in the royal house, over against the gate of the house.*

ויהי ביום השלישי ותלבש אסתר מלכות ותעמד בחצר

בית־המלך הפנימית נכח בית המלך והמלך יושב על־

כסא מלכותו בבית המלכות נכח פתח הבית:

Starting with the fifth letter in the fourth word, counting every second letter from left to right spells *shilhuv;* שלו מלחוב, which means *prosperity (security)...rapture.*

Starting with the first letter in the tenth word, counting forward every 11th letter spells *the rapture; ha'natzal;* הנצל, which means *the snatching up.*

Starting with the second letter in the eighth word, counting in reverse every eighth letter spells *hurry with excitement to Yeshua (Jesus); chush l'ah Yeshua;* חוש הל ישוע. The adjacent letters at the same ELS spell *the bridegroom; ha'chatan;* החתן. Also, *the bride; ha'kalah;* הכלה is encoded at 24-ELS.

Here again, we have insights that symbolize the rapture, bride, and groom. Notice that Esther went up to the king's house on the third day. This is similar to Exodus 19:16 and Hosea 6:1-2, where we find parallel insights alluding to the rapture. We see Esther as a type, or symbol, of *the bride of Christ—the King—this symbol foreshadowing our future, when we shall go up to our heavenly King's* throne in the rapture.

This is but a small portion of Scripture that relates to the rapture. Esther prepared herself before she was presented to the king; likewise, *we* must prepare ourselves with every breath and thought we have, before *we* are presented to *our heavenly King, Jesus the Messiah!*

Could this be the time of the rapture and the second coming, but separated by at least seven years? No one knows but the Lord Himself, so we must wait until that great day when we shall appear with Him in glory. In light of this, read and reflect upon the verses that follow.

1 John 3:1-3. (1) *Behold, what manner of love the Father hath bestowed upon us, that we should be called the sons of God: therefore the world knoweth us not, because it knew him not.* (2) *Beloved, now are we the sons of God, and it doth not yet appear what we shall be: but we know that, when he shall appear, we shall be like him; for we shall see him as he is.* (3) *And every man that hath this hope in him purifieth himself, even as he is pure.*

John is telling us that we are *now* the inherited *sons of God*. This means that whatever God's provisions for our spiritual needs, He has given those things unto us *now and forever. There is only one way that we could possibly acquire the benefits that God has for us, and that is through the shed blood of the Lord Jesus Christ.*

The most frequently asked question concerning the coming of the Lord is: *When will the rapture take place? Will there be a rapture of the living and dead at some future date—before, during, or after the Tribulation [time of Israel's trouble]?* The New Testament book of Revelation answers these questions once and for all, and it is also validated by the *Tanakh,* which is the Hebrew Old Testament.

Revelation 4:10-11. (10) *The four and twenty elders fall down before him that sat on the throne, and worship him that liveth for ever and ever, and cast* [threw] *their crowns before the throne, saying,* (11) *Thou art worthy, O Lord, to receive glory and honor and power: for thou hast created all things, and for thy pleasure they are and were created.*

This scene takes place around the throne of God in heaven before the *Tribulation.* How do we know this? Jesus is opening the seals of the *tribulation period* in chapter six, after the scene in heaven with the twenty-four elders. Notice that the twenty-four elders have received their rewards at this time. *The crowns symbolize that the time of rewards has come.*

Again, read what the apostle Paul has to say about our rewards or crowns. *Henceforth there is laid up for me a crown* [reward] *of righteousness, which the Lord, the righteous judge, shall give me at that day: and not to me only, but unto all them also that love his appearing* (2 Timothy 4:8).

Three areas of thought in this Scripture need to be viewed in a new and invigorating way.

1. The apostle Paul was not to receive his crown at his death, but would have to wait until the appearing (coming) of Jesus the Messiah.

2. Jesus is the righteous Judge. Therefore, this must be the judgment of the believers at the general resurrection. It is called the *bima;* בימה; *judgment,* which is *a platform for conducting judgment.*

3. We shall receive our rewards at the same time Paul does. This event will take place at the coming (appearing) of the Lord.

A friend of mine once told me that the elders surely *must* be some of those who were resurrected after Jesus was. The question I have with this reasoning is why the rewards (crowns)? We, with them, shall receive rewards at the same time, according to the apostle Paul. What Jesus showed the apostle John was yet to take place in the future.

Read carefully all the details above in Revelation 4:10-11. Men are referred to as *elders,* but *never* as angels. (Also read 1 Chronicles 24.) The elders have their rewards, so one must conclude by this that the rapture has taken place prior to the opening of the seals in Revelation 6, which introduces the tribulation period. This gives us enough evidence to believe in the pre-tribulation rapture.

In Revelation 5, the apostle John was perplexed because no one was found worthy to open the seals that introduce the time of Jacob's trouble (tribulation). In fact, he broke down and wept. The awesome scene described is very enlightening.

Revelation 5:5, 9-10. (5) *And one of the elders saith unto me, Weep not: behold, the Lion* [Messiah] *of the tribe of Judah, the Root of David, hath prevailed to open the book, and to loose the seven seals thereof.* (9) *And they sung a new song, saying, Thou art worthy to take the book, and to open the seals thereof: for thou wast slain, and hast redeemed us to God by thy blood out of every kindred, and tongue, and people, and nation;* (10) *And hast made us unto our God kings and priests: and we shall reign on the earth.*

The emphasis is on the believers from every nation who are in heaven singing the song of redemption before the seals of the tribulation are opened. One must conclude that the rapture has taken place; otherwise, why are we in heaven singing the song of redemption? One more note concerning those who resurrected after Jesus came out of the grave: Those dead believers were *not* from every kindred, tongue, people, and nation in the world, but concentrated in the area of the Middle East.

The tribulation period of seven years is a time of the *wrath of the Lamb; the wrath of God; the wrath of Almighty God; and the vengeance of the Lord on ungodly people.*

1. The wrath of the Lamb.

Revelation 6:16-17. (16) *And said to the mountains and rocks, Fall on us, and hide us from the* face of him *that sitteth on the throne, and from the wrath of the Lamb:* (17) *For the great day of his wrath is come; and who shall be able to stand?*

2. The wrath of God.

Revelation 15:1. *And I saw another sign in heaven, great and marvelous, seven angels having the seven last plagues; for in them is filled up the wrath of God.*

3. The wrath of the Almighty God.

Revelation 19:15. *And out of his* [Jesus'] *mouth goeth a sharp sword, that with it he should smite the nations: and he shall rule them with a rod of iron: and he treadeth the winepress of the fierceness and wrath of Almighty God.*

4. The days of vengeance.

Luke 21:22. *For these be the days of vengeance, that all things which are written may be fulfilled.* This refers to the time of the tribulation (Jacob's trouble).

We believers are *not* appointed to the wrath of God. However, we are currently under a relentless attack from the wrath of Satan. Nevertheless, he shall not prevail, because *greater is He that is within us than he that is in the world.*

1 Thessalonians 1:9-10. (9) *For they themselves show of us what manner of entering in we had unto you, and how ye turned to God from idols to serve the living and true God;* (10) *And to wait for his Son from heaven, whom he raised from the dead, even Jesus, which delivered us from the wrath to come.*

1 Thessalonians 5:9-10. (9) *For God hath not appointed us to wrath, but to obtain salvation by our Lord Jesus Christ,* (10) *Who died for us, that, whether we wake or sleep, we should live together with him.*

Seven

THE SEVENTH DAY

n Genesis, referring to the sixth day of creation, the encoded phrase, *Son of Israel;* בר־ישראל, is at seven-letter increments. The code for Israel starts in the Hebrew phrase, *the sixth day;* יום הששי, and runs through the seventh day when God ceased from His labors. Also, every 50th letter spells *greatness to Israel;* אל־רב־ישראל. This encoded phrase does the same thing; it overlaps from the sixth day into the seventh.

When considering the day-for-a-thousand-years concept (2 Peter 3:8), we can better understand that Israel will be a nation in the sixth day and will survive into the seventh day. In other words, at about the six thousandth year she will become a nation again, after many centuries of wandering from place to place and the Lord brings her back to the promised land. This concept brings us to this present age, when Israel became a nation again in 1948 and the Jews are, in fact, in their own land. This whole thought is Messianic in nature and refers to the Seventh Day (the one thousand year) reign of the Messiah on earth with head-quarters in Jerusalem. In order for this to be fulfilled, the Lord

Jesus must return to earth as promised and set up His magnificent kingdom.

When God rested on the seventh day, He ceased from all His accomplishments concerning the immediate creation. This is a picture of the *Feast of Tabernacles; Chag Sukkot;* חג סכת, when the whole world will experience the Messianic kingdom, where true peace will prevail. Within the record of the seventh day in Genesis 2 is encoded the name of Jesus at 70-ELS, which is the number of completion and perfection.

Starting from the Hebrew phrase in Genesis 2:1, *the heavens; ha'shamayim;* השמים, the name of *Jesus; Yeshua;* ישוע is encoded at 70-ELS. This hints at the idea that at the dawning of the Seventh Day, Jesus will return from heaven to bring Israel to her rightful place, which God had originally designed. The adjacent letters at 70-ELS spell *Creator; Borai;* בורא. Also, the adjacent letters at 2 x 70 (140) spell *Messiah; Mashiach;* משיח and *Creator; Borai;* בורא.

These phenomenal insights, revealed through the codes, tell us that Jesus the Messiah is the Creator of all things. He will create wonderful, new things in Israel and for the whole world. These new creations will take place when the kingdom is set up at the end of the seventh year of the seventy prophetic years, as prophesied in Daniel 9.

Not only will Israel be blessed during this 1,000-year reign of the Lord on earth, but all the nations of the world that from year to year come to Jerusalem to celebrate the Feast of

Tabernacles. It seems more feasible that every nation in the world would send their delegations during this time, because it would be very difficult for all the billions of people on earth to descend on Jerusalem at the same time.

For the last one hundred years or so, God has made available different methods of communication, such as the telegraph and teletype. Eventually, we progressed to the radio as a means of sending messages around the world. Since the end of World War II, television and satellites have been used to convey instant coverage of many different events. Today, we have the satellites and Internet, which connects us on a global scale with millions of computers at lightning speed.

These marvels of the twentieth and twenty-first centuries are being used by ministries throughout the world to send the Gospel. Overnight, because we can access these brilliantly designed inventions, millions upon millions of souls have been added to the kingdom of God as a result of the efforts of dedicated emissaries for the Lord Jesus Christ. In spite of some of the most vile abuses of these technologies, God's people are using them to proclaim the Good News, especially with the satellite ministries.

All these high-speed means of travel and communications are controlled by intricately designed computer systems utilized by God's people as well as by the secular world, bringing to pass the prophecy of Jesus in Matthew 24:14: *And this gospel of the kingdom shall be preached in all the world for a witness unto all nations; and then shall the end come.*

Isaiah 9:6-7. (6) *For unto us a child is born, unto us a son is given: and the government shall be upon his shoulder: and his name shall be called Wonderful, Counselor, The mighty God, The everlasting Father, The Prince of Peace.* (7) *Of the increase of his government and peace there shall be no end, upon the throne of David, and upon his kingdom, to order it, and to establish it with judgment and with justice from henceforth even for ever. The zeal of the LORD of hosts will perform this.*

The comparable Scriptures tell us additional information concerning this wonderful Child and Son who has been given to us, and who shall set upon the throne of David, governing us during the Seventh Day, the Feast of Sukkot (Tabernacles) that will last for one thousand years.

Micah 5:2-4. (2) *But thou, Bethlehem Ephratah, though thou be little among the thousands of Judah, yet out of thee shall he [Messiah] come forth unto me that is to be ruler in Israel; whose goings forth have been from of old, from everlasting. (3) Therefore will he give them up, until the time that she which travaileth hath brought forth: then the remnant [all Israel] of his brethren shall return unto the children of Israel. (4) And he shall stand and feed in the strength of the LORD, in the majesty of the name of the LORD his God; and they shall abide: for now shall he be great unto the ends of the earth.*

The prophet has identified the nation, town, and tribe into which the Messiah would be born, and that He would be the ruler in Israel. He came from eternity, outside of time and space, and He is the Son of God and of Israel. He would be born of a woman of God's choosing and would grow up in the admonition of the Lord, according to the Torah (Law).

In the verses from Micah, the Lord has encoded the name of the Messiah and His earthly mother and stepfather. Along with these insights, He has meticulously placed other codes that give us some additional information concerning the Messiah.

Micah 5:2. Starting with the second letter in the seventh verse, counting in reverse every 49th letter spells *Jesus; Yeshua;* ישוע. Adjacent to it, but at 48-ELS, is *Mary;* מרים and *Joseph;* יוסף.

There are other outstanding encoded insights found in this same area, giving us abundant proof of the Holy Spirit inspired Word of God.

Micah 5:1. Starting with the third letter in the sixth word, counting forward every 46th letter spells *the appointment (Feast) of my Servant; mo'aid Ovadi;* מועד עבדי.

Micah 5:5. Starting with the fifth letter in the ninth word, counting in reverse every 53rd letter spells *appointment of Jesus; mo'aid Yeshua;* ישוע מעד. This explains that God's appointed Servant is none other then the Lord Jesus Christ.

The royal genealogy of Boaz through David is also encoded in this same text at very low ELS, and they are (1) Boaz; בעז; (2) Obed; עבד; (3) Jesse; ישי; (4) David; דויד. This genealogy is verified in the Kinsman Redeemer's book of Ruth, the fourth chapter.

Boaz was a type of Messiah who portrayed the part of a kinsman redeemer when he took Ruth, who was a Moabite, for his wife. The Scroll of Ruth is a fascinating love story, which is a type of the Bride of Messiah (Christ), who was purchased by Boaz. Boaz and Ruth had a son named Obed, who fathered Jesse. Jesse's eighth son was King David, who also was a type of Messiah, the King of Israel. Encoded within the first chapter is an insight that reveals the name of the Messiah and one of His offices.

Ruth 1:8. Starting with the fourth letter in the tenth word, counting in reverse every 12th letter spells *the appointed King Jesus; Ha'Shait melek Yeshua;* השת מלך ישוע. Perhaps the number twelve has to do with the twelve tribes of Israel.

So you can readily see that in every Scripture throughout the Bible, referring in some way to the coming Messiah—His first coming, the rapture, and second coming—His name is encoded within that text. This can be corroborated from Genesis through the last book of the Bible.

The prophet Daniel was given various prophecies that would be fulfilled in his lifetime, but there were many that referred to the very end of the age. Of these many prophecies, the ninth chapter stands out, because there was given to him a time element for the fulfillment of these heavenly insights that God revealed unto him. Although he did not understand all of the prophecies, the Lord did give him clear understanding concerning many of them.

Daniel 9:24-27. (24) *Seventy weeks are determined upon thy people and upon thy holy city, to finish the transgression, and to* *make an end of sins, and to make reconciliation for iniquity, and to bring in everlasting righteousness, and to seal up the vision and prophecy, and to anoint the most Holy. (25) Know therefore and understand, that from the going forth of the commandment to restore and to build Jerusalem unto the Messiah the Prince shall be seven weeks, and threescore and two weeks: the street shall be built again, and the wall, even in troublous times. (26) And after threescore and two weeks shall Messiah be cut off, but not for himself: and the people of the prince that shall come shall destroy the city and the sanctuary; and the end thereof shall be with a flood, and unto the end of the war desolations are determined. (27) And he shall confirm the covenant with many for one week: and in the midst of the week he shall cause the sacrifice and the oblation to cease, and for the overspreading of abominations he shall make it desolate, even until the consummation, and that determined shall be poured upon the desolate.*

The prophet Daniel tells us that the Messiah would be cut off in death, but not for Himself. From the time the commandment went forth to rebuild the walls and Jerusalem, all the way to the death of the Messiah would be 483 years. This happened exactly as prophesied by Daniel. The Lord Jesus was put to death at the very end of the 483 years. This leaves us with seven additional years before the whole prophecy would be fulfilled. This seven years will be completed in the proper time, which will be at the very end of this age.

Daniel was talking about the Messiah being cut off; then he

skips over to the end of the age and reveals the end of the prophecy. The week (שבוע) in Hebrew represents the last seven years before the kingdom age.

Many years ago I did an analysis of the book of Daniel, especially the ninth chapter. I meticulously examined the Hebrew Masoretic Text for any information that would corroborate the seven year-tribulation doctrine. To my amazement, the numbering system from the Hebrew text verified this seven years. Remember, this portion of the book of Daniel was dictated to him by the Lord's angel.

Daniel 9:26b. *And its end shall be with the flood, and ruins are determined, until the end shall be war.* [Hebrew Interlinear]

וקצו בשטף ועד קץ מלחמה נחרצת שממות:

When I added together the numerical value of each letter, I was surprised about what God has placed in His Word. The total value of all the above letters equals 2,520. This is the same amount of days that the tribulation will last when calculating according to the Hebrew calendar. Seven years times 360 = 2520.

To verify the week (seven years) about which Daniel is speaking, we need to go to Genesis 29:20, 27-28. (20) *And Jacob served seven years for Rachel: and they seemed unto him but a few days, for the love he had to her. (27) Fulfill her week, and we will give thee this also for the service which thou shalt serve with me yet seven other years. (28) And Jacob did so, and fulfilled her week; שבע [seven years]: and he gave him Rachel his daughter to wife also.*

When using the prophetic calendar of Israel, we have 360 days in a year. Counting from the time the decree went forth by King Artaxerxes in Ezra 7:11-26 (March 14, 445 B.C.), counting 173,880 days (69 x 360 years) brings us to the time of the Passover in the first century A.D. This was the time when the Messiah was crucified, thereby, fulfilling to the very day and the time that the Messiah would be cut off. We still have one more week (seven years) of the original prophecy to be fulfilled. I believe we are coming into that time period as you read this book.

The prince who shall come is not the Messiah, but the false messiah who will strengthen a covenant with Israel for one week (seven years). In the middle of the week, he shall cause the sacrifice to cease and set himself up in the Temple to be worshipped as God. This time period is called the time of Jacob's trouble, or the tribulation.

The time from the cutting off of the Messiah to the beginning of the tribulation when the false messiah comes was not revealed to anyone. This is usually called *the age of grace* or *the Church age*. Just prior to the time of trouble, the blood-bought, born-again saints will be removed according to the prophet Isaiah, Malachi, and the New Testament writers.

There are several Scriptures in the Old Testament that verify this doctrine. The *caught up* (rapture) truth is revealed in the fifth chapter of Genesis and in various other verses throughout the Bible. This is not a new doctrine, as some have proposed, but as old as the heavens themselves. Enoch, the seventh from Adam, is a type of those faithful believers who walk with God. As it was with Enoch, so shall it be again when the Lord descends from heaven to call us to Himself.

Genesis 5:22-24. (22) *And Enoch walked with God after he begat Methuselah three hundred years, and begat sons and daughters:* (23) *And all the days of Enoch were three hundred sixty and five years:* (24) *And Enoch walked with God: and he was not; for God took him.*

Hebrews 11:5-6. (5) *By faith Enoch was translated that he should not see death; and was not found, because God had translated him: for before his translation he had this testimony, that he pleased God.* (6) *But without faith it is impossible to please him: for he that cometh to God must believe that he is, and that he is a rewarder of them that diligently seek him.*

The following are various codes that are located in the area of Genesis 5:22, where it talks about Enoch walking with God.

1. Jehovah; יהוה at + 26 ELS.

2. Jesus; ישוע at + 26 ELS.

3. Messiah; משיח at -14 ELS.

4. To be snatched (caught) up; ינצל at + 73 ELS.

The prophet Isaiah refers to the time of birth pangs, great fury, the escape, the resurrection, and the second coming.

Isaiah 26:17—27:1. (17) *Like as a woman with child, that draweth near the time of her delivery, is in pain, and crieth out in* *her pangs; so have we been in thy sight, O LORD. (18) We have been with child, we have been in pain, we have as it were brought forth wind; we have not wrought any deliverance in the earth; neither have the inhabitants of the world fallen. (19) Thy dead men shall live, together with my dead body shall they arise. Awake and sing, ye that dwell in dust: for thy dew is as the dew of herbs, and the earth shall cast out the dead. (20) Come, my people, enter thou into thy chambers, and shut thy doors about thee: hide thyself as it were for a little moment, until the indignation be overpast. (21) For, behold, the LORD cometh out of his place to punish the inhabitants of the earth for their iniquity: the earth also shall disclose her blood, and shall no more cover her slain. (1) In that day the LORD with his sore and great and strong sword shall punish leviathan the piercing serpent, even leviathan that crooked serpent; and he shall slay the dragon that is in the sea.*

There are many encoded words and phrases that directly relate to the One who will hide us from the fury that is coming. The Hebrew word, *the snatching up; the rescue;* הנצל, is encoded at least five times in the above text.

The birth pangs always refer to the time of great trouble, the tribulation, when Israel will be delivered from leviathan, the piercing serpent, the dragon in the sea of people. This is the devil himself, who will be bound and cast into the bottomless pit. Isaiah 27:1 and Revelation 12:2-3 are closely related.

Revelation 12:2-3. (2) *And she being with child cried, travailing in birth, and pained to be delivered.* (3) *And there appeared* *another wonder in heaven; and behold a great red dragon, having seven heads and ten horns, and seven crowns upon his heads.*

The seven heads are the seven different empires.

1. Egypt

2. Assyria

3. Babylon

4. Medo-Persia

5. Greece

6. Rome

7. Revised Rome

The ten horns represent the last Gentile empire that will come out of the territory of the previous empires. We have been especially watching the boundaries of the ancient Roman and Grecian empires since 1948. The ten toes of Daniel have been on the rise since that time, but the final formation of the ten nations takes place about the same time as when the tribulation begins. All of these prophecies will be fulfilled before the Lord returns the second time, when He destroys this blasphemous military, religious, and political system that is being controlled by Satan himself.

By the time Alexander the Great invaded Israel during his military campaigns, he had conquered most of the known world of his day. At his death, the four generals under him divided his Grecian Empire into four sections. The prophet Daniel received a revelation concerning the end-time of these kingdoms and what would happen in the last days. The antichrist (false messiah) was revealed as well as his prosperity and his end.

Daniel 8:22-25. (22) *Now that being broken [Alexander], whereas four stood up for it, four kingdoms shall stand up out of the nation, but not in his power.* (23) *And in the latter time of their kingdom, when the transgressors are come to the full, a king of fierce countenance [antichrist], and understanding dark sentences, shall stand up.* (24) *And his power shall be mighty, but not by his own power: and he shall destroy wonderfully, and shall prosper, and practice, and shall destroy the mighty and the holy people.* (25) *And through his policy also he shall cause craft to prosper in his hand; and he shall magnify himself in his heart, and by peace shall destroy many: he shall also stand up against the Prince of princes [Jesus]; but he shall be broken without hand.*

There is no question about the time of the fulfillment of these prophecies, which will take place at the end of this age as we know it. In the second chapter, Daniel sheds additional light on this subject. God revealed to Daniel in a vision the four empires that will exist from the time of Babylon to the end of the age. The fourth kingdom, the Roman Empire, will produce from its feet ten toes, which represent ten nations that exist during the final fulfillment of these prophecies.

These ten nations will be controlled by the antichrist, who will control the whole world. But the Lord also gave Daniel a picture of the bitter end of this ungodly alliance, which will be this vital information about strategic planning by the United Nations.

It is believed by some insiders that this organization plans to divide the world into ten separate regions, which will be under the UN's complete control.

Daniel 2:34-35. (34) *Thou sawest till that a stone was cut out without hands, which smote the image upon his feet that were of iron and clay, and brake them to pieces.* (35) *Then was the iron, the clay, the brass, the silver, and the gold, broken to pieces together, and became like the chaff of the summer threshing floors; and the wind carried them away, that no place was found for them: and the stone that smote the image became a great mountain, and filled the whole earth.*

There are several insights encoded in this section of the Hebrew text that reflect the *Stone that is cut out without hands.*

Daniel 2:34. Starting with the second letter in the 18th word, counting forward every 26th letter spells *Christ; Messiah;* משיח. The adjacent letters, but at seven-ELS, spell *the house of David; Ha'Beit le'Da'vid;* הבית לדוד. This is a Messianic term referring to the tribe (Judah) from where the *Stone that is cut out without hands* would come.

These Scriptures need to be read in conjunction with Daniel 12. They are speaking of the same time element, the end of the age when the Messiah sets up the kingdom.

Daniel 12:7. The Hebrew phrase, *and sware by him that liveth for ever,* reveals from the encoded insights the name of the Messiah from Daniel, chapter 2.

Daniel 12:7. Starting with the fifth letter in the 15th word, counting in reverse every 26th letter spells *Jesus; Yeshua;* ישוע.

The prophet has brought us to the place in the Scripture that gives us undeniable proof that Jesus is the Messiah, and that He will bring to pass all these end-time prophecies when He returns the second time.

I want to draw your attention to one more in the series of Scriptures referring to the end-time, the return of Christ, and the setting up of the Messianic kingdom. This is the answer to the disciples' question, *"Lord, will thou at this time restore again the kingdom of Israel?"* (Acts 1:6).

The prophet Zechariah refers to the end of days when all nations gather against Jerusalem and there seems to be no hope of survival.

Zechariah 14:1-4. (1) *Behold, the day of the LORD cometh, and thy spoil shall be divided in the midst of thee.* (2) *For I will gather all nations against Jerusalem to battle; and the city shall be taken, and the houses rifled, and the women ravished; and half of the city shall go forth into captivity, and the residue of the people shall not be cut off from the city.* (3) *Then shall the LORD go forth, and fight against those nations as when he fought in the day of battle.* (4) *And his [Jesus'] feet shall stand in that day upon the mount of Olives, which is before Jerusalem on the east, and the mount of Olives shall cleave in the midst thereof toward the east and toward the west, and there shall be a very great valley; and half of the mountain shall remove toward the north, and half of it toward the south.* (5) *And ye shall flee to the valley of the mountains; for the* *valley of the mountains shall reach unto Azal: yea, ye shall flee, like as ye fled from before the earthquake in the days of Uzziah king of Judah: and the Lord my God shall come, and all the saints with thee.*

I believe this sums it up sufficiently. The prophet said the Lord God shall return and bring all the saints with Him. This is the second coming of the Lord Jesus with all believers from every generation.

Revelation 19:14-16. *(14) And the armies which were in heaven followed him [Jesus] upon white horses, clothed in fine linen, white and clean. (15) And out of his mouth goeth a sharp sword, that with it he should smite the nations: and he shall rule them with a rod of iron: and he treadeth the winepress of the fierceness and wrath of Almighty God. (16) And he hath on his vesture and on his thigh a name written, KING OF KINGS, AND LORD OF LORDS.* The fine linen, white and clean, is the righteousness of the saints (Revelation 19:8).

This event will introduce the world to the Feast of Tabernacles, the Seventh Day, as recorded in Zechariah 14, thereby fulfilling the seventh day of creation in Genesis 2:1-3.

Zechariah 14:16. *And it shall come to pass, that every one that is left of all the nations which came against Jerusalem shall even go up from year to year to worship the King, the Lord of hosts, and to keep the feast of tabernacles.*

Without a doubt, the Bible is referring to those who shall have been caught up to heaven at the time of the rapture of the believers and their return to earth at the second coming. Are you going to be in that number of blood-washed believers? If you are not sure, this is the time to call upon the name of the Lord and to ask Him to forgive you and save you from your sins. *He will surely answer that prayer request, because the Lord Himself says that it is not His will that any should perish.*

APPENDIX

Spiritual truths we all should agree on about Jesus the Messiah (Yeshua ha'Mashiach).

Romans 10:8-13. (8) *But what saith it? The word is nigh thee, even in thy mouth, and in thy heart: that is, the word of faith, which we preach;* (9) *That if thou shalt confess with thy mouth the Lord Jesus, and shalt believe in thine heart that God hath raised him from the dead, thou shalt be saved.* (10) *For with the heart man believeth unto righteousness; and with the mouth confession is made unto salvation.* (11) *For the scripture saith, Whosoever believeth on him shall not be ashamed.* (12) *For there is no difference between the Jew and the Greek: for the same Lord over all is rich unto all that call upon him.* (13) *For whosoever shall call upon the name of the Lord shall be saved.*

When Yeshua established His assemblies, they all were messianic congregations, consisting of Jew and Gentile alike. The Hebrew word for assembly is *qehillah;* קְהִלָּה. Another word that is used for *fellowship* is *chavrah;* חָבְרָה. Since the times of the early believers, much has changed in each congregation of believers. The reason for this is that many different people from many different nations and walks of life have come into the kingdom of God through simple faith in our Savior, Jesus Christ (Yeshua haMashiach). The differences that exist in various congregations demonstrate that it is the grace of God that is shed abroad from one end of this world to the other, thereby, encompassing all people, regardless of their ethnic backgrounds.

Many people go from congregation to congregation, trying to find an assembly that agrees with them. It is probable that they will not locate one that suits their doctrinal point of view. If you do find a congregation that teaches these twenty-five basic articles of faith, I feel you should settle there and be a part of its growth. When you join yourself with an assembly, allow your spiritual inner person to grow in the revelation of our Lord and Savior.

1. Yeshua is the Word of God made flesh.

John 1:1-3, 14. (1) *In the beginning was the Word, and the Word was with God, and the Word was God. (2) The same was in the beginning with God. (3) All things were made by him; and without him was not any thing made that was made. (14) And the Word was made flesh, and dwelt among us, (and we beheld his glory, the glory as of the only begotten of the Father) full of grace and truth.*

2. Born of a virgin.

Matthew 1:23. *Behold, a virgin shall be with child, and shall bring forth a son, and they shall call his name Immanuel, which being interpreted is, God with us.*

3. His perfect, righteous life.

2 Corinthians 5:21. *For he hath made him to be sin for us, who knew no sin; that we might be made the righteousness of God in him.*

4. Yeshua, the miracle worker.

John 2:11. *This beginning of miracles did Jesus in Cana of Galilee, and manifested forth his glory; and his disciples believed on him.*

5. Healer of your body, soul, and spirit.

Luke 4:18-19, 40-41. (18) *The Spirit of the Lord is upon me, because he hath anointed me to preach the gospel to the poor; he hath sent me to heal the broken-hearted, to preach deliverance to the captives, and recovering of sight to the blind, to set at liberty them that are bruised,* (19) *to preach the acceptable year of the Lord.* (40) *Now when the sun was setting, all they that had any sick with divers diseases brought them unto him; and he laid his hands on every one of them, and healed them.* (41) *And devils also came out of many, crying out, and saying, Thou art Christ the Son of God. And he rebuking them suffered them not to speak: for they knew that he was Christ.*

6. Yeshua is God's perfect love manifested.

Romans 8:35-39. (35) *Who shall separate us from the love of Christ? shall tribulation, or distress, or persecution, or famine, or nakedness, or peril, or sword?* (36) *As it is written, For thy sake we are killed all the day long; we are accounted as sheep for the slaughter.* (37) *Nay, in all these things we are more than conquerors through him that loved us.* (38) *For I am persuaded, that neither death, nor life, nor angels, nor principalities, nor powers, nor things present, nor things to come,* (39) *Nor height, nor depth, nor any other creature, shall be able to separate us from the love of God, which is in Christ Jesus our Lord.*

7. The Lamb of God.

John 1:29. *The next day John seeth Jesus coming unto him, and saith, Behold the Lamb of God, which taketh away the sin of the world.*

8. Yeshua was arrested for crimes He did not commit.

Isaiah 53:5-9. *(5) But he was wounded for our transgressions, he was bruised for our iniquities: the chastisement of our peace was upon him; and with his stripes we are healed. (6) All we like sheep have gone astray; we have turned every one to his own way; and the Lord hath laid on him the iniquity of us all. (7) He was oppressed, and he was afflicted, yet he opened not his mouth: he is brought as a lamb to the slaughter, and as a sheep before her shearers is dumb, so he openeth not his mouth. (8) He was taken from prison and from judgment: and who shall declare His generation? for he was cut off out of the land of the living: for the transgression of my people was he stricken. (9) And he made his grave with the wicked, and with the rich in his death; because he had done no violence, neither was any deceit in his mouth.*

9. He was executed on the Feast of Pesach.

John 18:28. *Then led they Jesus from Caiaphas unto the hall of judgment: and it was early; and they themselves went not into the judgment hall, lest they should be defiled; but that they might eat the passover [pesach].*

10. He descended into hell to preach to the spirits in prison.

Ephesians 4:9-10. (9) *(Now that he ascended, what is it but that he also descended first into the lower parts of the earth? (10) He that descended is the same also that ascended up far above all heavens, that he might fill all things.)*

1 Peter 3:18-19. (18) *For Christ also hath once suffered for sins, the just for the unjust, that he might bring us to God, being put to death in the flesh, but quickened by the Spirit. (19) By which also he went and preached unto the spirits in prison.*

11. He was resurrected on the third day.

Luke 24:4-8, 44-48. (4) *And it came to pass, as they were much perplexed thereabout, behold, two men stood by them in shining garments: (5) And as they were afraid, and bowed down their faces to the earth, they said unto them, Why seek ye the living among the dead? (6) He is not here, but is risen: remember how he spake unto you when he was yet in Galilee, (7) Saying, the Son of man must be delivered into the hands of sinful men, and be crucified, and the third day rise again. (8) And they remembered his words. (44) And he said unto them, These are the words which I spake unto you, while I was yet with you, that all things must be fulfilled, which were written in the law of Moses, and in the prophets, and in the psalms, concerning me. (45) Then opened he their understanding, that they might understand the scriptures, (46) And said unto them, Thus it is written, and thus it behooved Christ to suffer, and to rise from the dead the third day: (47) And that repentance and remission of sins should be preached in his name among all nations, beginning at Jerusalem. (48) And ye are witnesses of these things.*

12. He overcame death, hell, and the grave.

Revelation 1:17-18. (17) *And when I saw him, I fell at his feet as dead. And he laid his right hand upon me, saying unto me, Fear not; I am the first and the last: (18) I am he that liveth, and was dead; and, behold, I am alive for evermore, Amen; and have the keys of hell and of death.*

1 Corinthians 15:51-58. (51) *Behold, I show you a mystery; We shall not all sleep, but we shall all be changed, (52) In a moment, in the twinkling of an eye, at the last trump: for the trumpet shall sound, and the dead shall be raised incorruptible, and we shall be changed. (53) For this corruptible must put on incorruption, and this mortal must put on immortality. (54) So when this corruptible shall have put on incorruption, and this mortal shall have put on immortality, then shall be brought to pass the saying that is written, Death is swallowed up in victory. (55) O death, where is thy sting? O grave, where is thy victory? (56) The sting of death is sin; and the strength of sin is the law. (57) But thanks be to God, which giveth us the victory through our Lord Jesus Christ. (58) Therefore, my beloved brethren, be ye steadfast, unmovable, always abounding in the work of the Lord, forasmuch as ye know that your labor is not in vain in the Lord.*

13. Many of the First Covenant believers who died were resurrected immediately after His resurrection.

Matthew 27:52-53. (52) *And the graves were opened; and many bodies of the saints which slept arose, (53) And came out of the graves after his resurrection, and went into the holy city, and appeared unto many.*

14. He was seen by many in His resurrected body.

1 Corinthians 15:3-8. (3) *For I delivered unto you first of all that which I also received, how that Christ died for our sins according to the scriptures; (4)And that he was buried, and that he rose again the third day according to the scriptures: (5) And that he was seen of Cephas, then of the twelve: (6) After that he was seen of above five hundred brethren at once; of whom the greater part remain unto this present, but some are fallen asleep. (7) After that, he was seen of James; then of all the apostles. (8) And last of all he was seen of me also, as of one born out of due time.*

15. After forty days He ascended into heaven.

Acts 1:3, 9-11. (3) *To whom also he showed himself alive after his passion by many infallible proofs, being seen of them forty days, and speaking of the things pertaining to the kingdom of God: (9) And when he had spoken these things, while they beheld, he was taken up; and a cloud received him out of their sight. (10) And while they looked steadfastly toward heaven as he went up, behold, two men stood by them in white apparel; (11) Which also said, Ye men of Galilee, why stand ye gazing up into heaven? this same Jesus, which is taken up from you into heaven, shall so come in like manner as ye have seen him go into heaven.*

16. He promised to return for the living and the dead believers.

1 Thessalonians 4:13-18. (13) *But I would not have you to be ignorant, brethren, concerning them which are asleep, that ye sorrow not, even as others which have no hope. (14) For if we* *believe that Jesus died and rose again, even so them also which sleep in Jesus will God bring with him. (15) For this we say unto you by the word of the Lord, that we which are alive and remain unto the coming of the Lord shall not prevent them which are asleep. (16) For the Lord himself shall descend from heaven with a shout, with the voice of the archangel, and with the trump of God: and the dead in Christ shall rise first: (17) Then we which are alive and remain shall be caught up together with them in the clouds, to meet the Lord in the air: and so shall we ever be with the Lord. (18) Wherefore comfort one another with these words.*

17. He promised we would go with Him to heaven.

John 14:1-3. *(1) Let not your heart be troubled: ye believe in God, believe also in me. (2) In my Father's house are many mansions: if it were not so, I would have told you. I go to prepare a place for you. (3) And if I go and prepare a place for you, I will come again, and receive you unto myself; that where I am, there ye may be also.*

18. Yeshua is the Baptizer of the Holy Spirit and fire.

Matthew 3:11. *I indeed baptize you with water unto repentance: but he that cometh after me is mightier than I, whose shoes I am not worthy to bear: he shall baptize you with the Holy Ghost, and with fire.*

Acts 2:1-4. *(1) And when the day of Pentecost was fully come, they were all with one accord in one place. (2) And suddenly there came a sound from heaven as of a rushing mighty wind, and it filled all the house where they were sitting. (3) And there appeared unto* them cloven tongues like as of fire, and it sat upon each of them. (4) And they were all filled with the Holy Ghost, and began to speak with other tongues, as the Spirit gave them utterance.

19. We are to be baptized with water into Yeshua Ha'Mashiach.

Matthew 28:19. *Go ye therefore, and teach all nations, baptizing them in the name of the Father, and of the Son, and of the Holy Ghost.*

Acts 2:38. *Then Peter said unto them, Repent, and be baptized every one of you in the name of Jesus Christ for the remission of sins, and ye shall receive the gift of the Holy Ghost.*

20. Yeshua, the Messiah, our King and High Priest.

Hebrews 7:17, 25-26. *(17) For he testifieth, Thou art a priest for ever after the order of Melchizedek. (25) Wherefore he is able also to save them to the uttermost that come unto God by him, seeing he ever liveth to make intercession for them. (26) For such an high priest became us, who is holy, harmless, undefiled, separate from sinners, and made higher than the heavens.*

21. Yeshua is LORD of Lords and KING of kings.

Revelation 17:14. *These shall make war with the Lamb, and the Lamb shall overcome them: for he is Lord of lords, and King of kings: and they that are with him are called, and chosen, and faithful.*

22. Yeshua is the Creator.

Colossians 1:16-19. *(16) For by him were all things created, that are in heaven, and that are in earth, visible and invisible,* *whether they be thrones, or dominions, or principalities, or powers: all things were created by him, and for him: (17) And he is before all things, and by him all things consist. (18) And he is the head of the body, the church: who is the beginning, the firstborn from the dead; that in all things he might have the pre-eminence. (19) For it pleased the Father that in him should all fulness dwell.*

23. Yeshua and the believers will reign on earth for 1,000 years.

Revelation 20:5-6. *(5) But the rest of the dead lived not again until the thousand years were finished. This is the first resurrection. (6) Blessed and holy is he that hath part in the first resurrection: on such the second death hath no power, but they shall be priests of God and of Christ, and shall reign with him a thousand years.*

24. Israel will be completely restored in the promised land.

Ezekiel 37:24-28. *(24) And David my servant shall be king over them; and they all shall have one shepherd: they shall also walk in my judgments, and observe my statutes, and do them. (25) And they shall dwell in the land that I have given unto Jacob my servant, wherein your fathers have dwelt; and they shall dwell therein, even they, and their children, and their children's children for ever: and my servant David shall be their prince for ever. (26) Moreover I will make a covenant of peace with them; it shall be an everlasting covenant with them: and I will place them, and multiply them, and will set my sanctuary in the midst of them for evermore. (27) My tabernacle also shall be with them: yea, I will be their God, and they* shall be my people. (28) *And the heathen shall know that I the LORD do sanctify Israel, when my sanctuary shall be in the midst of them for evermore.*

25. Yeshua is the LORD (Jehovah) Eternal.

Without the resurrection of Yeshua haMashiach, none of the above blessings would benefit us. There would be no hope in this world or the world to come. Praise the LORD, all you people! Praise His holy name!

Revelation 1:4-8. (4) *John to the seven churches which are in Asia: Grace be unto you, and peace, from him which is, and which was, and which is to come; and from the seven Spirits which are before his throne; (5) And from Jesus Christ, who is the faithful witness, and the first begotten of the dead, and the prince of the kings of the earth. Unto him that loved us and washed us from our sins in his own blood, (6) And hath made us kings and priests unto God and his Father; to him be glory and dominion for ever and ever. Amen. (7) Behold, he cometh with clouds; and every eye shall see him, and they also which pierced him: and all kindreds of the earth shall wail because of him. Even so, Amen. (8) I am Alpha and Omega, the beginning and the ending, saith the Lord, which is, and which was, and which is to come, the Almighty.*

If ye then be risen with Christ [Mashiach], seek those things which are above, where Christ sitteth on the right hand of God (Colossians 3:1).

Look up! God will guide your feet; lest, looking down you may stumble.

BIBLIOGRAPHY

Baugh, Dr. Carl, and Dr. Clifford Wilson. *Footprints and the Stones of Time.* Oklahoma City: Hearthstone Publishing, Inc., 1992.

Green, Jay P. Sr., general editor and translator. *The Interlinear Hebrew-Aramaic Old Testament.* Peabody, Massachusetts: Hendrickson Publishers, 1985.

Jeffrey, Grant R. *The Signature of God.* Toronto: Frontier Research Publications, Inc., 1996.

Mahan, Rev. W. D. Valleus' notes—"Acta Pilati," or Pilate's report to Caesar of the arrest, trial, and crucifixion of Jesus. *The Archko Volume.* New Canaan, Connecticut: Keats Publishing, Inc., special contents copyright, 1975.

Missler, Chuck. *Cosmic Codes.* Coeur d'Alene, Idaho: Koinonia House, 1999.

Mozeson, Isaac E. *The Word: The Dictionary That Reveals the Hebrew Sources of English.* Northvale, New Jersey; London, England: First Jason Aronson Inc. edition, 1995.

Rambsel, Yacov. *His Name Is Jesus: The Mysterious Yeshua Codes.* Toronto: Frontier Research Publications, Inc., 1997.